A WOMAN WRAPPED IN SILENCE

May, 2004

To Marsha with love.
You and Our Blessed Mother
have a special relationship
I pray you will make
time to read about her
in this book.

Aunt Dorothy

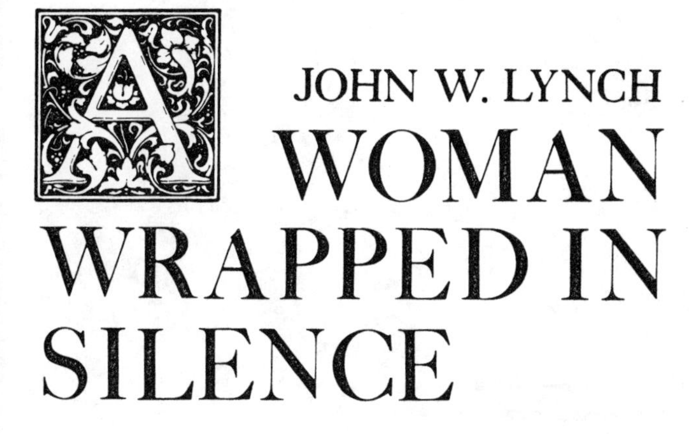

JOHN W. LYNCH

A WOMAN WRAPPED IN SILENCE

PAULIST PRESS
New York/Mahwah, N.J.

ISBN 0-8091-1905-6

Published by Paulist Press
997 Macarthur Boulevard
Mahwah, New Jersey 07430

www.paulistpress.com

Printed and bound in the
United States of America

TO MY

FATHER AND MOTHER

A WOMAN WRAPPED IN SILENCE

A WOMAN WRAPPED IN SILENCE

HIS was a little child who knew not man,
Nor life, nor all the needed frauds of life,
Nor any compromise, and when she turned
To raise the earthen jar, and faced the airs
Of Spring, she smiled for young security,
And she was glad. These were her own, these lanes
Of Nazareth. She'd known the slope and feel
Of them for all her years, and they had known
Of her, and she was walking now and was
Familiar, and the well she sought not far
Beyond the clustered houses was so old
It had become a part of permanence.
The sky around it was so clear, serene
With blue, and framed with hills that had been hers
For always, and which lifted up a silence
She had loved. These thresholds were her friends,
These white walls leaning, and the narrow doors,
And she could watch the shadows and the slant
Of sun, and turn a corner so, and hear
The farther crowing of a cock, and guess
That in the marketplace were dusty sheep
She could not hear; and passing on, she marked
With deeper care that from an opened window
Rose the sound of psalms. She was at home.
These few streets and the ruts in them were home,
And she was sure, and young, and now the others
At the well had called to her, and said
Among them it was Mary who had come.

They mentioned Joseph to her with a smile
And nod, and one remarked that she had seen
Him at a friend's house yesterday, and that
His work was moving on, and he had plans
He'd spoken of, and that he'd asked for her.

They turned with understanding in their eyes
And looked to her. She was a woman here
Who'd made a bond with Joseph. She could sense
Their knowing that, they saw her now as his,
Belonging, with a place and name declared
And set and sealed beyond the need to think
It could be ever altered or would change.
She held that in her thoughts. She'd made a bond
With Joseph. He had given her his word
And she'd consented. She had made a bond.
And after she had moved away and placed
The filled jar to her shoulder, and had gone
A distance up the little sloped return,
It came to her that this content, this ease,
This quiet in her was not of the hills,
Or roofs, or streets that were her childhood's paths,
But was of Joseph. Joseph was her peace.
He was her home, and holding in her now,
His name was warm and strong and innocent
Of fears. She could be confident of him,
She could be glad for Joseph, she could trust . . .

And then she was remembering the day
He came to pledge to her. Joachim,
Her father, had stood forward solemnly.
Behind him, Mary Cleophas and all
The rest of kinsfolk, cousins, and the friends

Who were as dear. And he had come, and was
Not bold, and offered Joachim the gift
Of *mohar,* and had said it was a sign.
And afterward, the lesser gifts of *mattan*
He had brought for all to share in him.
They were not rich, his gifts, and he had spoken
Softly, and she could remember how
His voice had trembled, and he'd said that prayers
Were on his heart.

O, Joseph, Joseph! She
Had known there would be prayers. And when the time
Of waiting ended, and procession formed
To lead her to his house, she'd have no fears.

And smiling in the peace that mantled her,
She reached her father's door again and stepped
Within to old repeated tasks and cares
That for these brief months still would be her own.
No change had come because the plighted word
Of Joseph had been said, and villagers
Could recognize she was betrothed to him.
The spinning must be done, the weaving threads
Be caught and mended, and the knots untied,
The pans and ovens filled with bread, the crusts
Must still be hoarded, and the counted needs
Of poverty be met. She walked upon
The stairs and watched for Joachim, and called
Across the street to neighbors and received
Their news, and when the day was bright, she closed
The shutters to the sun. She woke, and slept,
And moved, and bound her hair up in a braid.
She saved the moments out that gave her heart

To God, as she had always done, and all
Around her, Nazareth was small and old
And settled on its hills, and kept the old
Ways it had learned. She was a young girl here. . . .

But when across the years we see her so,
Our generation finds it hard to think
Of her as one with us. Our stains have made
Us hesitant, and sad remembrance curls
And turns within to slow the prideful binding
To ourselves, as if the very claim
Could soil in her the grace whose essence is
It is not soiled. This name is benediction
On our blood, defence and refuge, hope
And harbor, and our one fair memory
Of innocence, and we have known too long
Its silence on the world's wild clamoring
Not now to know this name is uttered prayer
And not a name.

And yet, the gifts that were
To weigh her heart will find already there
Bewilderment, and seated fears, and sight
That moved no farther than her vision ran,
And God gave her to see. Not true to think
Her tears were not as salt as tears may be,
And not as real. It is not true to say
Her sweetness made a cushion for the blows
That fell on her, and left her warmed and snug
Against the starkness of the staring night.
This voice could laugh, and sob, and sing, and cry:
This was a woolen garment that she wore
About her tired shoulders, and the hands

That brushed the weight of hair from off her brow
Were roughened with the water jars, and knew
The feel of sunlight and the form of bread.

Not strange is this, and we have always known
It true, that she was one with us, and yet,
We've built so many towers in our skies,
So often flung the great stones up for her
To ease the heart's full need, and be a praise
To stand above the years' long pondering;
So often have we turned the litanies,
Strung out so many garlands, while her bells
Have called to us, and kneeling we have sighed
In such dear confidence . . .

We scarce remember
Now that once this name was spoken softly
In a time before the Aves rang.
Perhaps across some threshold it was said,
So casually, by one who called to her,
"Mary." Then, she might have turned and come,
Obedient from where the children played
Together in the dusk: and no one knew
That more was said than just a young girl's name.

No, not true to think that then her feet
Were visibly upon the serpent's head,
And stars ringed visibly about her brow.
Except for gentleness and modesty,
The grace she held in fullness, was as grace
We hold, a silent gift, unknown, if knowing
Be the shattering of earthly molds,
And loosing of the need for watchfulness.

No deep, relentless tide of ecstasy
Swept over her, to carry her beyond
The world she knew, and make her stranger here.
The dawn was cold, and in the dark, the wind
Still spoke of other dawns, and all her days
Were labor and were vigilance. And peace
That made its quietness in her was peace
God gave, since she had made a place for it
By tired hands and a heart that did not tire.

His way with men has been to take men's way,
And that's the glory and the scandal both . . .
O, not the thunders and the lifted gates
He chose, and not exotic retinue
To bring Him flaming through the breathless towns
With swift compulsion and command, not this,
But briefest pausing in the pulse of life,
With all our old simplicities unmarred,
With no rejections of the flesh we bear,
The hearts we love with, and the pain we know.
He slept our sleep, and with us dreamed our dreams.

And when the hour had come that was to move
The long days onward up to Bethlehem,
Until a faint new cry should break across
Our air that had not heard such cry before,
Weighted with ungarnered potencies,
High portent unreleased, and tremulous
With mercies still unsaid, a moment paused
Above a quiet place, and found, just this,
A woman wrapped in silence, and the seed
Of silence was her heart that tried to give
All that it held to give, and ever more.

Spilled all about her, pooled in radiance,
The guardian brightness of God's favor lay,
Like light, too luminous to bear the trace
Of shadow, too intense, too strong for sight.
No vision here is ours. Nor Gabriel's,
Who, shaded in his sanctity, was sent
To stand here, lonely and apart, to speak
In whisper that which only God could see.

Hail, full of grace, the Lord is with thee: Blessed art thou among women.

O, Luke had words to tell, but Luke's good words
Are faltering, and halt before they lead
Beyond the outer margins of the light:
And only this we know, and knowing now
Keep higher hopes and on our race may hold
A stronger blessedness: O, only this . . .
Within the light, the mercies of the Three
Were offered unto her: Who made all power,
Paused, and suppliant, was powerless . . .

The Holy Ghost shall come upon thee, and the power of the most High shall overshadow thee. And therefore also the Holy which shall be born of thee shall be called the Son of God. And behold thy cousin Elizabeth, she also hath conceived a son in her old age: and this is the sixth month with her that is called barren; because no word shall be impossible with God.

Not, "Aye," returned: not, "Aye, for all the tribes
And all the worlds await." But secretly,
Uneager, prideless, unafraid, the brightness

Flamed to greater radiance, and then . . .

Behold the handmaid of the Lord, be it done to me according to thy word.

* * * *

This is conclusion, and the fires that scorched
The Prophets' lips, the old consuming fires
That burned in Israel's blood might now be cooled;
For prophecies are ending, and the dreams
That throbbed above the great unfinished music
Of the psalms are quieted, and psalms
At last resolve, like chords that come to rest.
This is fulfillment, and upreaching hands
May now be folded, and the long desires
That beat, half heard in need, through all the veins,
May now be eased. New testament is made,
New visitation, and a full new world
That holds much more of mystery, and more
Of consequence than that which answered first
From nothingness.

And yet the quiet here
Retains no trace of great archangel wings,
And now that all the words are said that waited
To be said, the voices leave no trail
Of echo after them to tell that once
They spoke. Dust is floating undisturbed,
And from a distance comes the muffled noise
Of moving wheels and sound of daily things.
A moment came, and that is all, a moment
Came and passed, and in the passing left

A young girl here who was not now alone.
This was not she who lifted up her head,
And yet it was, and crowded days that stretch
Beyond will still be bound for her in sun
And in the dark. Her steps will fall upon
The dust and leave an imprint there, and tasks
Will weary her. Dedicate, and now
So utterly bequeathed, her strengths are yet
Her strengths.

This is God's chosen way with men,
To take men's way: and so the streets she walks
And all the roads, the shepherds and the shepherds'
Sheep, the winds, the firelight, Israel's hills,
Will find just this, no more, a woman plain
Upon the earth, and in her arms, a Child.

II

WHEN soundless voices and the hidden words
Were gone and only evening filled the room
With light, when sign of miracle as yet
Moved not beyond this secret heart it chose,
And she who was not now alone, stood lonely
With her Own, in this, first aftertime
One there was who heard her speak, and looked
More kindly and more closely than the rest.

Joseph did not need to wait for reasons
To be here, but on this night he came
More swiftly since her father sent for him,
And what he kept within permitted him
To see in her that which all the others
Could not see.

Joachim had said
He was to speak against her leaving them
In so much haste, to add his words against
Some sudden journey to Elizabeth
She seemed disposed to make. But sitting near
The shadows, Joseph caught within her face
That which could not let him be too quick
In speaking.

What it was he did not know.
The light lay shaded in her eyes and dimmed,

And only at long intervals he saw
The rise of brightness that could not be dimmed
Nor longer held. Yet what it meant, he was
Not sure; whether of joy or pain or both
He could not guess, and he had lived too long
To find distinction easy. Only this
Was sure . . . whatever moved in her was sweet,
And somehow there was that which made him sense
The utter force of it, when quietly
She spoke again about Elizabeth.

Joachim was mindful of the journey's
Ardor and the length of road before
Accomplishment, which, he also said,
Could only find assistance in a child
Some younger than herself since none might ride
With her except that one best spared from them.
Not that he was contrary, or thought
Her so . . . however quick her wish was formed
For visitation. Kinsfolk ought to meet . . .
He loved Elizabeth . . . and she was old,
And on her face so many years were lined . . .
And in the past she'd done him kindnesses.
Elizabeth was now with child he'd heard.
He wondered if it would be well with her.
Perhaps she'd need of Mary. Aye. Perhaps . . .
And Zachary, her husband, was a priest
Of Levi. Joachim was proud of that . . .
That he was relative to one who served
So high before the Temple. Zachary
Would make her welcome . . . and the tones of pride
Rose stronger on his words, but not so strong
As in an observation later made

That royal blood of David graced his tribe . . .
And Joseph's tribe . . . and hence was cause for honest
Honor and rejoicing, that the tie
In Israel's King would not be lost to him,
Now that betrothal had been ratified.

Aye, that was true: espousal had been sealed,
And mention of it now made Joseph's heart
Rise up again and sent his glance to search
The shadows for her eyes that still were closed.
He could not see them, yet he had seen them,
And was content in hope and memory.

The feeling moved in him again that more
Lay hidden in her soft, repeated wish
Than what she said, or dared to let be said.
The depth of quick abstraction in her look,
The light, and then the shading of the light,
As if a sunrise sought concealing mists,
Or such a surge and conscious ebb the mind
Might know at what is undeserving dear.
So, quietly, he spoke, and did not see
The sudden movement of her gratitude
When favoring the journey and the haste,
He said it good to seek Elizabeth.

There was not more thereafter, save some talk
Of towns and roads, and friends along the roads,
Of cordial word, and gifts that she might bring,
And then departures, and the little lights,
The droning voices, and the dark had made
An ending.

And the silence sifted in,
And she might dream of more than even dreams
Would dare. . . .

* * * *

If eagerness would urge the patient feet
Beyond the pace they made, to stir the dust
Less leisurely, no one could know of it
Who saw them pass and marked how quietly
The veils enfolded her. And how unhurried
Moved the plodding beast beyond the gates.
Tradesmen crowded here, and Caesar's men,
Merchants, Jews, and carts and caravans,
Loud upon the roadway, cluttered, noisy,
Shouting for a space, and frightening,
Except that littleness and poverty
Could thread a small unnoticed passageway
Until Judea's kneeling hills had made
Again a refuge, and the winding path
Was quieter, and kind with loneliness.

Some shadows fleeting on a wayside hedge,
Faint sound of passage, and the tread of hoofs,
Moving figures, small against the sky,
And that was all . . . the hills had folded them.

This was the first of all the aftertime,
Closed and harbored in a virgin's hours,
A still, unbroken interim where songs
Were born and ghosts of songs to run a distance
Now no wider than her lifted heart,

Returning in unutterable exchange
Of secrecy. Inviolate. Unshared.
Yet mingling with the songs were gusts of fear.
For frailty. Of worth and need of worth.
Of Joseph now? Of Joseph and the bond?
And what of prayer or faltering caress
When He Who Is lay cradled in her arms,
And only her poor kingdom crowning Him?
But fears were fugitive, and if the song
Could dare to free itself, would be no more.

This was the first of all the aftertime,
And a long road was drowsy in the sun.
His was the sun! And His, the moving grass!
The hills were His, and every wisp of cloud
That wandered asked direction and His way!
His, the winds! The stir of wordless life!
The shimmer of the heat that brushed across
Her lowered eyes! And a name she heard recalls
Itself among the hoofbeats on the road.
"Elizabeth . . . Elizabeth . . . for Him . . ."

The roof that was the end of all the roads
For her, lay like a friend that called beyond
Some little trees, to move remaining steps
More quickly. Yet no evidence was plain
To give assurance of prophetic word
She'd heard of it, to tell it sheltered one
Who held a sign. The whitened walls were still.
The vines were hushed. The shuttered windows, closed.
Aloofness brooded here, and eager steps
Were slowed, reluctant, at a door that held
Such silence. Breathlessly she entered in.

Her eyes, quick searching, were a soundless plea,
And from the muted tumult of her heart,
A single word that was more cry than name . . .
"Elizabeth!"

If there were need of more,
It was not here. A voice to one who heard
The voice, and then, O, first response, and first
Of all the prayers her ears would hear of earth!
O, word of grace, and name first called that wakes
The years to tribute! Salutation. Blessing.
Prelude and release for virgin song.

Blessed art thou among women, and blessed is the fruit of thy womb. And whence is this to me, that the mother of my Lord should come to me? For behold as soon as the voice of thy salutation sounded in my ears, the infant in my womb leaped for joy. And blessed art thou that hast believed, because those things shall be accomplished that were spoken to thee by the Lord.

Of Zachary, no word: yet kindred word
His tears could give for stronger utterance.

And now, the gift that trembled unreleased,
Was free. Was free! The heart could cry of it,
And know no violation in the cry.
The voice could lift and whisper ecstasy
The hours had hid, and glad unfettered words
Were free to break across the muted lips
In winged release that was as music soaring
To a sudden freedom in an ease
That curved and swung away to silver flight

More artless for its long held pondering.
The joy of it! The utter gift of it!
The silence ended. Out of it, her song!

My soul doth magnify the Lord: And my spirit hath rejoiced in God, my Saviour. Because he hath regarded the humility of his handmaid.

O, fragrance of an incense burned to Him,
Now rising from her heart's rich thurible.

For behold from henceforth all generations shall call me blessed. Because he that is mighty hath done great things to me: and holy is his name.

To spread His sweetness out beyond the flame
That is her own, for lesser fire to take,
And then return above the kindling blaze.

And his mercy is from generation unto generation, to them that fear him. He hath showed might in his arm: he hath scattered the proud in the conceit of their heart. He hath put down the mighty from their seat, and hath exalted the humble. He hath filled the hungry with good things: and the rich he hath sent empty away.

To be another cloud, again the fire
That goes before His chosen, leading on
To where new kingdoms come to humbleness.

He hath received Israel his servant, being mindful of his mercy. As he spoke to our fathers, to Abraham and to his seed for ever.

And drifting, pause above sad Israel,
To be a sign that God had not forgot:
For prophecies are ended, and the dreams.

* * * *

The days will keep these echoes and the song
Will be forever singing in the years.
But now, the sound is lost, and in a space,
The day is dull again, and Zachary
Could only hear a woman and a child
Who shyly spoke of things that women say.

III

SOME there are who say her uttered song
Is summary of all the words that fell
Along the moments of unfolding hours
To make a constant praise arise for Him
Between her young lips and Elizabeth's.
It would not be too strange if this were true,
For here were cloister and a first retreat,
Brief pause of time, and sheltering from need
Of more than time; and dear awareness here
Might grow unhindered, and unbrokenly,
The vigils might be kept, so safe, so still,
So guarded by the gates, and two that also
Knew, without invasion, could be near.

But now the gates have swung, and slow return
Has made an end of sheltered days, and when
The hills had hid the roof that harbored her,
And distances are less to Nazareth,
Fears that had been fugitive awhile
Return to rustle on the edge of peace
Like small insistent birds that will not hush . . .
Of Joseph and the weeks that still remained
Before the bond became a common roof . . .
And then the fears were not insistent wings,
But winds that rose relentlessly and swept
The sure defences of her prayers to frighten
Peace and make their gusty storming seem
The single certain thing. Until a word

Remembered from some other fears had come
To her again: "O, be it done to me."

And so was quiet entrance made again
To old, unvanished places, and the cares
She left were given her, and words were said,
And kinsfolk only knew a little girl
Who had been gone, returned. But there was one
Who knew he'd waited longer than the rest.

The beam's clean curling and the rasping sound
That Joseph's plane was making slowed, and stopped,
And listlessly, his hand ran down the edges
He had made, as if some lack or need
Of industry had come to him, yet more
As if the mind were absent on a task
Involving other trueness than demand
Of work.

So seldom stilled before, the blade
Was frequent in its silence now, and pauses
Came that left the pleasant smell of wood
The only tie to keep within the place
Of labor, thoughts that were not yet content.
"It is . . . it must be so," he said, or thought
He said. And was he not a carpenter?
And therefore used to seeing what was there?
Skilled in exactitude, in lines and lengths
And angles on his boards, a man who knew
The accuracies and kept them as his craft
Had always kept them since the world's emergence?
He was not a man to dream, or think
He'd seen an evidence not truly seen.
No, this could not deceive him now . . . and soon

The slow, thin edging of the plane again
Aroused him, and it was the thoughts that ceased.
But then, another pause, and with a quick
Impatient move, abandonment of work.
The plane lay idle, and his calloused hand
Made absent twistings of the curls of wood,
And then destroyed them. What it was he'd seen,
Or seemed to see, and what the meaning was
Could not be carried in the one same mind
With sanity! And then the press of it
Made Joseph vaguely turn and seek again
Whatever sureness or relief was left
To him in sharpened edges and in tools
That were like other selves.

But not for long,
For now his mind cast up once more the wish
She'd strangely formed to see Elizabeth.
Why had that been? And why the length of weeks
Before return? Then it was . . . he thought . .
After this return . . . he dared to see
That which now he dared not think was seen.
Yet all distress and anguish could not hold
The lighting smile that came when he remembered
How accustomed he had grown to watch
For her, and follow with his very heart
The passage of her way along the street.
The smile had faded now . . . reluctantly
He'd seen, and through all protests, still must see
More plainly.

For a moment his distress
Turned in upon itself, and he was shamed

He could be so, and quickly willed to think
Of how much more he'd learned was in the world
Than that which could be measured and described.
Stronger things than timbers and the rules
He builded on: and more was here, unchanged,
And with its own sweet aura that could seem
More silver as the days brought sight of her.
Aye, modesty and gentleness were there
Within her lowered glance . . . and only that!
The sure serenity of blamelessness
Still shone, until a stronger name was needed
Than a lack of fault. It was as if
All purity had breathed a crystal air
For her to walk in. Or, as if a trace
Of all sweet prayer still clung to her as clouds
Of incense linger in a Temple court,
To keep awareness of a Presence there.
He'd sensed that many times before, but now
Around her moved much more than he had seen
At other times, and greater reverence.
That might be felt by blunter men than he.
But how . . . how dare to ask? And harm by thought?
To be more bold than ever soul would dare?
And yet, unwillingly, he still could see.

He'd heard of honor, and had judged of it
To be a worthy grace and dignity,
And one which might be worth the guarding well,
And so . . . but for the moment he was tired,
And left the contradictions unresolved,
Certain of his eyes, but yet more sure
Instinctive deference could not mislead.

The winds that were her fears were not content
To trouble waking hours in fitful gusts,
But set more fiercely in when night had come
To shut away distraction and the brave
Defences raised of old, familiar things.
She'd sought the darkness once, and welcomed it
For solitude, so grateful that the speech
Of day was ended, and her lifted prayers
Were measured only in the pulses' quiet
Beating and the slow, sweet length of time.
But there were moments now when opened eyes
Could only stare into the dark and find
No more than darkness and anxiety.
He did not know. Joseph did not know!
She felt his look upon her with the kindness
Almost gone from it! She'd speak to him?
But what were words to use, and dare she speak
The mercies God had asked to hide through her?
If this might only fall on her who knew
Each wound, gratuity. But what of Him
Who would be born of her? What of Him?
Then like a worn and tired wanderer
Who finds some sudden shelter in a storm,
She thought again: "He hath received His servant
Israel" . . . and there was peace.

Until
A swift reflection came. A burden now
Was hers and word was pledged that she would care
For Him . . . was this implicit in the pledge?
Then fiercer winds were in the dark and beat
To thunderous tumult that could not be borne
Except her stronger prayers could make a silence,

And the place of silence was her heart
That tried to give all that it held to give,
And ever more.

Decisions must be made:
And if the men who make them hold the grace
To think there may be error where they judge
So bravely, then they make them quietly,
And keep away too great a noise. And Joseph
Was a man who knew whatever word
Must now befall, his was the part to use
Such reticence he'd not deny his love.
His manhood only asked to bless and spare,
Yet now, the anguish that he might do harm.
The laws were harsh on those who broke a bond,
And welt or bruise was farthest from his wish,
So far, that faintest thought of it was torment.
Stay decision . . . if delay could heal . . .
Yet that aroused again the issue's swirl,
And there had been enough of pondering.
He knew a way . . . he'd heard of it . . . to break
In secret, quietly, espousals made.
Yes, that was best. A word of kindness said
To Joachim . . . that there might be no more . . .
No more of bonds. Tomorrow he should speak.
And then, not gladly, but as one whose task
Is ended, Joseph sighed, and shut a door
Behind him, and the hopes . . .

But while he thought on these things, behold the Angel of the Lord appeared to him in his sleep, saying: Joseph, son of David, fear not to take unto thee Mary thy wife, for that which is conceived in her is of the Holy Ghost. And she shall bring forth a son: and thou shalt call his name Jesus. For he shall save his people from their sins.

And now he *knew* what he had always known.
All purity had breathed a crystal air
For her to walk in, and the trail of all
Sweet virtue lingered for a fragrant cloud.

* * * *

What source we have of knowledge of her days
Is sparing, and has left us many days
Still veiled, and if there is enough to find
What Joseph found, and a few dear treasured words,
We must have more to lead us where our love
Would seek to go. And there is one sweet place
That distant watching eyes could fondly wish
To see and ponder on. Did Joseph come,
And with his sobs seek pardon for his fears?
And did he see how, suddenly, his love
Was greater than he knew and could be carried
Now along new pathways with his prayers?
God's kingdom now was four, and claimed again
Another life to be with Zachary,
To listen with Elizabeth, and then
With her to serve. O, glad, he was for strength,
And glad for honor, and for name, and glad
His hand was skilled enough to fashion walls
And build the smallness of a crib that now
Would cradle more than all the world could hold.
Dreams of all his fathers fell on him
In one bright dream, and all bright hopes were clear.

We may not know for sure, and yet, and yet,
May we not see how quietly he came
And spoke no word. And Mary saw him come,
Finding a new thing shining in his eyes.
And when quick tears of gladness and relief
Were done, she saw him kneel, lift up his hands,
Two hands that held invisibly, his life.
She may have reached her own pale fingers out
And found them . . . calloused, generous and *strong*.

IV

THE measure of the days since Gabriel's word
Had fallen on the silence of her heart,
Was not so great as left accounting now
Too difficult, except that she had learned
That days may run to other measuring,
And some few moments be a span of years.
A newer heaven and a dearer earth
Had made the sweet accustomed prayers to rise
Beyond themselves and stir an eagerness
That broke through sleep in quickened, sudden life,
Reluctant to endure the night's full pause,
Until it seemed the days before were far
By distant lifetimes, or were lived by one,
A wordless stranger, who no longer lived.

What hallowed plans there were, what deep designs
Conceived and set for Him Who was to come
From long eternity, she did not know.
And yet, the passing days and slow unfolding
Of the consequence had made it plain
His was a simple way, and more might not
Be asked of her than quiet, simple tasks
That women found habitual and dear.
No obvious, angelic courtiers
Attended her, and she remembered now
How she had come upon a blossom, white,
And growing near the road from Nazareth.
Her shadow fell on it, and she had paused

To note there was not change, that still it felt
His Presence only in the sun's abundance,
And the winds.

Aye, this was certain now,
And Joseph's coming gave new evidence
Of undisturbed and sweet simplicity.
The Will that mightily had moved to mark
Its hour, the summoning of angels told
To speak again the accents of the Voice
That once had called from out the whirlwind's depths,
Fulfillment of the Ancient Covenant,
And sudden harking to the patient pleas
That Israel's years had sobbed, had only caused
A woman named Elizabeth to bow
Her head, and made a carpenter to walk
More softly in the dawn to lift his hands.

And that was all. No more. The gentle ways
Were still unshattered, and the paths that lay
Before her were familiar ways to her,
And to such watchers as might look to find
Her walking them, and if intriguing stars
Were gathering a burst of flame for Him,
It had not shone above the nearer skies.

Joseph now had spoken, that was all,
And then a word was said in reference
To sealed betrothal that the solemn bond
Be recognized, and such procession formed
And progress made unto the bridegroom's roof
As was the custom when the interval
Of waiting was complete.

Expectant folk
Had judged it obvious remaining rites
Implicit in the bond already sealed,
Be now observed, and a few kind words were said,
And busy stir of preparation made
A house less quiet now than usual.

There was some fitting grant of festiveness,
Some singing, and a pace or so of slow
Procession, tapers lighting, and a branch
Of fresh cut leaves to wave in friendly hands.
Yet such display was not enough to pause
Or alter much a town's preoccupation
Nor disturb it, and whoever stopped
To look could only see that this was more
Subdued than most processions, and a soft
Aloofness brooding here had made it seem
As if their thoughts were elsewhere and could find
No great concern in present ritual.
And then the kinsfolk and the townsmen turned
Again to more engrossing enterprise
That had been laid in favor of politeness
And a moment's casual interest.

But walking now by Joseph's side, she knew
A quiet peace, more certain and more sure
Because so swiftly sent, and then as one
Who only wondered whence would come the peace,
She rested, and observed the longer shadow
That his figure made ahead of her.
It moved but slowly, like the shade it was,
And trustingly she moved beside and knew
His heart for harbor, and his arm for strong

Protection; and the long brave humbleness
That shaped his virtues and had made him worth
The word that had been said to him, released
Her heart to freedom and the virgin thoughts. . . .

He might be born, and see the stars through eyes
That were her eyes in Him! And might she trace
Her features in the molding of His brow?
Hear her voice in His, and know the need
He had of her, and uttered in a cry?
And she . . . and . . . she might sing for Him at dusk!
Might sing, but no, she could not dare this dream . . .
But yet, it was a mother's need to sing . . .
And then a song the world has never heard,
Rising in the faintest strains of distant
Loveliness had moved along the silver
Shining of her dreams, like light returned
Within a purer light, until it came
To her unfrightened. Caroling of angels'
Praise, and love that lifts to lullaby
Became as one, and blended for a fragile
Music that was hers and only hers.
She caught at it, and sweetly let it rest
Among the kindred graces of her soul
To hold it for a secret solitude
With Him Who was to hear, and still must hear.

She might hold Him! Hardly had she thought
Of that . . . but she might hold Him! And a hand
Might close upon her fingers, or be tangled
In her hair, and she might feel His breath . . .

My soul doth magnify the Lord: . . . Because he that is mighty hath done great things to me: and holy is his name.

But then the singing of procession ceased,
And with a gentle bow, she smiled on one
Who came to wish her well.

And very near,
The man named Joseph walked with her. "Fear not,
O, fear not, Joseph" . . . he had heard and knew
It now for kindly speech that bravened him,
And let him dare to tread this road, and then,
A sudden, fierce, responding dedication
Flamed to fire and claimed so utterly
His days, his labors, all that he might build,
That there was left in him no strength ungranted
To remain his own: "Fear not . . . fear not."
And then his thoughts were measured in his pace.
Step, by step, by step. And once he raised
His eyes and saw a faintest light in hers.
He lowered them and knew that she had smiled
The words an angel granted her to say
To him, and to the wistful years . . . "Fear not."

V

THE patterns formed to prelude ended now
And all the fears and dreams, and she was one
Who'd come unto a sheltered place to rest.
To wait now, that was all, and these were walls,
And this a household waiting. Days were filled
With it, and passing time was pulsed and vibrant
With a hushed expectancy that knew
No need of other hopefulness and made
No quest of more.

There was not overmuch
Of speech, and only muted reference
To that which was, and that which was to come.
This household set, unsigned and undistinguished
With some others on a village hill,
Moved on as other village households moved.
A fire to tend, and earthenware to scour,
Lamps to trim and keep, and threads to draw,
While old words fell . . . about the morning blue,
And of the rains. But old worn words were not
As others spoke. Behind them lay the waiting
To be heard whatever had been said.
And usual tasks were silhouette against
Awareness, flaming like a constant light
That haloed with its own significance
The cares that were for her but cares for Him.
To come. To go. To pull the shutters in.
To mark the daybreak hour and dark. To speak,

But always now to know this was but waiting.
Waiting . . .

It has not been granted us
To watch, but were there moments when her heart
Broke through to cry again of humbleness?
And tried to search some virtue that she thought
Unfrayed? And was there not a pause between
The pulsebeats when the thoughts dared not to run
Beyond the next faint movement, and the breath
Was caught for fear, and half a world of women
Seemed more gracious and more fair than she?

Aye, sometimes at the grateful end of day,
When hands were resting in the quiet dark,
Joseph knew, and wordlessly, he knelt
With her beneath the stars and let the cool
Clean fragrance of the night enfold the prayers,
And if the distant shouting of some child
Called out to other voices, laughing, then
He knew again, if she but lifted up
Her head, or seemed to listen for a sound
Unheard, the hours he guarded now were waiting . . .
Waiting . . .

* * * *

Then a word came with the iron
Of empire forged in it: the lords of earth
That sent the triremes out from Rome had thundered
Of enrollment. Lands and provinces,
They'd said, and men and citizens and slaves.

An unaccustomed peace had strangely come
About the frontiers, closed the war god's gate,
And it had seemed a time for reckoning.
And so Cyrinus, prince and governor
Of sorts, had caught the thunder of the lords,
And sent it down the villages to break
From house to house until the thunder fell
Across this little roof at Nazareth.

And Joseph also went up from Galilee out of the city of Nazareth into Judea, to the city of David, which is called Bethlehem: because he was of the house and family of David, to be enrolled with Mary, his espoused wife, who was with child.

We've heard of Bethlehem: it is a name
We speak more tenderly, nor is it uttered
Only with the lips. It is a name
That drifts to us from out remembered years,
And holds within the sound and lilt of it
A sweetness that we may not drone away.
Its syllables are stars, and songs, the good
Simplicity of shepherds, and the word
Is linked to all the innocence we've saved.
But now we must forget this Bethlehem,
And hear it as a place some distance off,
The name a town had, and a cause for some
Reflection and an anxious pondering
Of roads and plans for reaching it.

And then,

A door was closed behind them, and the sound
Was loud in isolated emphasis

Against the stillness and the dawn's cold fog,
And afterward, two shadow figures dimly
Moved beneath the greyness, and reluctant
Hoofbeats clattered near. A woolen shawl
And wrappings clutched together for the cold
Enveloped her. She may have trembled once
Or twice, and pulled them closer, while her eyes
Were straining, and she saw that in the mists
The small transparent drops were clustering
Upon the matted back of Joseph's beast.
Some low words spoken quickly, and the first
Few steps are taken on the road, and when
A final glance had shut away this house
That had been hers, the echo of her movement
Fades to silence. But it is not lost,
This sound of gentle passageway, this tread,
This lonely fall of steps is beating back
Through all the buried years of Israel's hope,
To stir remembered dreams and to awake
The visions that had heard this sound in dreams.

And thou, Bethlehem Ephrata, art a little one among the thousands of Juda: out of thee shall he come forth unto me that is to be the ruler in Israel: and his going forth is from the beginning, from the days of eternity.

The day was early, yet a townsman seeing
Them was not surprised. They would be gone
Some little time. It was that recent law
About enrollment that the Romans made.

* * * *

This distance is a space that still remains
For all accounting. Ninety miles, grown neither
Short nor long for time, and marked across
The face of maps, still there to be observed
And judged a somewhat lengthy pilgrimage.
So learnedly we say that frequent rest
And easy stages made it possible,
And since there is a due regard for guests
Among the Eastern peoples, they had known
No lack of friends or shelter on the way.
And yet for all dismissal, it is still
A lengthy road. And there were dust and rain,
And gusty winds to whip about her shawls.
Long passing caravans grown boisterous
And not too sweetly tempered, nor too pleased
With journeying, and when the press of prouder
Wayfarers grew close, it does not seem
Too much to think her glad for Joseph's hand
Against the bridle, nor to judge he sought
The margin places on the road, and walked
More firmly with his back against the beast
Lest it be frightened, or some wheel-cast mud
Rise up to strike against her gathered robe.
It's true enough, that they had often stopped,
And she had gone, as one among the rest
Of women then to find relief against
The road's fatigues, and when the fires were made,
She worked among them in the fading day.

Did they not know? Could they not feel the nearness?
Was there not a faint reluctance come
For old sad ways, and quick new gladness rising
In them, even though they could not trace

The Source? Already, some unheld reflection
Of the questing light that was to rest
Forever in His eyes, looked out from hers
As answering, she said: "To Bethlehem."

But now the darkness, and the fires were dimmed,
And there was only breathing and the stir
Of restless men, and then, as if the search
Had somehow been rebuke to Him, she closed
Her eyes, to open them, beyond the dark,
To find a light where there was only silence,
And the place of silence was her heart
That sought to give all that it held to give,
And ever more.

Afterward the road
Shook off the hills, and glad for wide release,
Flung out its freedom buoyantly between
The plains of Juda; and remembering,
They came unto the land, the land that leadeth
To Ephrata. Out beyond, the fields
Were broad, and sloped away beneath the skies,
And only little winds were whispering.
Here Ruth had walked to glean the scattered grain,
These were Rachael's fields, and here the son
That Jacob called the son of his right hand,
Cried out for her who could no longer cry,
And Jacob mourned, and stooped to bury her
Beside this road: and here had David watched
His father's flocks, and set his young face, eager
Towards the dreams.

It was not then fatigue
That slowed the steps and left them motionless,

Unheeding that the steady pace had ceased.
The unforgetting winds were whispering
Of older times that kept an older hope,
And Joseph, turning, did not think it strange
To find her veils were lifted, and her eyes
Were luminous and distant on the fields,
And when they closed again, he did not speak,
But only broke the silence with a pace
That had been paused a moment on the land
That leadeth to Ephrata.

A little while,
And then the day was slipping down behind
The dark, and clung there, like a crystal drop
Before it fell and shivered to the spent
And countless multitudes preceding it.
Could there be more than shadow in this night
Now coming on? O, was there here some haste
That pushed the light more hurriedly, as if
This were an ending era, and the last
Of days? Was an impatience reached among
Reliant stars to goad them swiftly on,
To touch at last a newer time they'd watched
Approaching since the rise of time? If so,
And if this light paled, conscious of conclusion,
Joseph did not seem aware of it,
And only saw a thickening of men
Upon the road, and urgency that raised
The pace of movement, fretful for an end
Of journeying. His own steps hurried so,
And tugged the lead rope tighter for the threat
Of shadows, and a glance of hers looked up
A moment fondly to the anxious lift

Across his brow. Then suddenly, the road
Was turning, and ahead, some clustered roofs,
White and crescent-shaped against a ridge,
Traced out a city that their fathers made
And left there, lonely in the years, to wait
Her passage through the gates.

And they had come

With humble anonymity to lose
Them in the others' hurrying, and press
Of dull confusion made it difficult
For her to catch what it was he must
Have said, when first they trod upon these stones.
A grace was in it, tenure, and a claim
That was not there before, and could not be
Except that she was there to hear. He turned
And called to her: "Mary. It is here.
This is Bethlehem."

And they had come,

And with them came the darkness of a night
Unchanged from other nights, that lighted windows,
Made the doors secure, and set men seeking
Fires and walls against the alien sky.
And was unchanged for them who asked a roof
And warmth and some small certainty of peace.

So now he pulled the bridle on a path
Well worn, ahead of him. It was not much,
This place of caravan, nor soft with comfort,
Yet a place to lay a mat, and light
A fire and feel that there were others near.
A kind of courtyard, square, but with a roof

Around the edges, and a gate to close
Behind the road. They could not ask for more.
But Joseph's eyes were hopeful as he stood
To wait an answer. Then he heard them say,
There was no room for them within the inn.

Lift up your gates, O ye princes, and be ye lifted up, O eternal gates: and the King of Glory shall enter in. Who is this King of Glory? The Lord who is strong and mighty: the Lord mighty in battle . . . the Lord of hosts, he is the King of Glory.

And . . . the Holy which shall be born of thee shall be called the Son of God. . . . And of his kingdom there shall be no end.

But it was true. Already many there.
There was no room for them within the inn.
And Joseph turned away.

To find again,
A woman wrapped in silence. Had she heard?
No sign appeared, nor stir of tranquil veil
To tell of it. Perhaps she had not heard.
Or was it that whatever rudeness spoke,
Whatever loss or lack of interest,
Colder and more harsh within the dark
Than rudeness, could not mar a calm grown deep
Beneath the weight of time since shadows came
To mark this night begun. What fear could reach
Within was not derived of words, nor meanings,
Nor a lack of roof, and now a love
Much older than the present peace, was masque

Lest Joseph judge she thought he'd somehow failed.
And if a tired droop bent down the worn
Sweet frailness of her shoulders, then the road
Had caused it, and it could not seem complaint.

But Joseph knew. And silence and the glance
That smiled to him could not shut out the need
For shelter that was yet unsaid. He knew!
And suddenly it rose in him again
What it was he knew, and what was here
Beseeching in the night. An innocence
That had been burnished flawless to return
All brightness, till the Inexhaustible
Had searched for her this last and utter grace
That left no more to give: then, choiring
Of seraphim had stilled, and in the hush
That ached along the last, far reaches past
The Throne, the word she gave in answer fell
Like blessedness that had not been before.
The burst of vaulting song resuming choirs
Had lifted, was a silence in the greater
Praise that she had spoken in the one
Brief sounding of her voice, and in the least
Of prayers that now were constant in her heart.
And he was guardian. Guardian!
Whose task to fear not, but to throw his life
About her as a cloak. To be a strength
Between her and the world's unsanctities.
To fend, and guard, and break the fall of harsh
Rejection. He had need of heartening.
And when a door was closed against his search,
And emptiness was all he had to bring,
She'd known the first of all her ministry.

He had not thought refusal was a word
Remaining in a language that had held
Her name. There had been much since he had dreamed
Of humbleness and joy. Of doubt of worth,
And fears, but not denial. But he'd heard
It said. So calmly, he had heard it said,
So firmly: No, there was no room for them.
He'd turned again. The fierce cry burned within
His throat. But it was stilled before it broke
Against the gate, and in the quietness
Her presence made, he found again the rope
That had been dropped, and strained his eyes to see
Beyond the darkness, and the lonely way.

Other searching then there may have been,
His voice uplifted hopefully to ask
Across the lighted space of other doors.
There may have been a weariness of words
To speak a first refusal many times,
And drive the dull pain deeper in his mind.
We do not know, and Luke has been content
To stop at one short sentence left to stand
Without adornment, sharpened as a blade.
But in whatever search, or lack of search,
He only found the night, and then a ridge
In black relief against the lighter sky.
Caves were here, and places where the shepherds
Climbed when rains swept down the pasture land.
And one of them was not too far beyond
The inn and was unclaimed. It had a roof
To spread, and some dry places deep within
Where there were straw, and broken timbers set
Against the rock, and had been, on occasion,

Shelter for an ass or ox whose owner
Was not rich, nor overscrupulous.
The face of it was open to the stars,
And to whatever winds might will to blow,
But when they came to it, they found it good
With silent welcome, and with loneliness.

Standing now before this place, she heard
No sound, except a vague, infrequent stir
Behind the darkness and the nearer sound
Of Joseph's searching, and the low hushed words
He afterward called back to say to her
He'd found a place within that was unsoiled.

The pause then was as brief as breath to breath,
A moment caught from out the flow of time,
And held before she answered, while her heart
Took up the shape this stable dimly made,
And pressed the outline in, indelibly.
Its height, its barrenness, the smell it had,
And how it seemed so lost between the world's
Great spaces, yet so good against remembrance
Of the courtyard and the littered inn.
And then she moved, and Joseph reached his hand
To guide the movement, and the flow of time
Was free again, except this folded moment
That she held to keep, unchanged.

A step
Or so, uncertain in the dark, some dust
That may have fallen at her groping hand,
And then there was no need of further steps,

Nor thoughts to run again beyond the present,
Dreaming what fair place be given Him,
Or what good habitation might be His.
And in the swift content that rested here,
There was renewal of a long surrender,
And enough to lift this little space
Above the earth's full worth, and make it dear
Beyond the walls of home.

A little girl
Had wandered in the night, and now within
The shadows of a broken stall, was waiting,
While the night winds and the breath of time
Were moving over her.

Of Joseph then?
O, did he rise and stealthily return
Before the cave's wide entrance, there to stare
Within the dark? And lift his eyes to search
The trembling stars? And did he feel the midnight's
Slow, sweet advent and the pulse of joy
That ached beneath the hours, as sharp as pain?
And did he mark again the barrenness
And with a craftsman's hand run sadly down
A length of broken beam? And suddenly
Did Joseph fall upon his knees and know
Our purest human helplessness, and hold
His heart the centre of a tide of sobs
That deepened, silently, lest she might hear
Who did not need to hear? And were there prayers?
Uncertainties? What happened here until
A cry came that had not been heard before?

The beat of pulses and the hush of heart
Had made a silence more intent within
Surrounding silence. Deepening of night.
The last pure poise of prayer, more still and wordless
In an utter distillate of prayer.
Starlight moving imperceptibly.
The drift of time. And then a moment's fall,
The last that we should know of loneliness.
A sigh, unheard within the dark, and then . . .

She . . . wrapped him up in swaddling clothes, and laid him in a manger.

Only that. The brief, sweet offices
Of motherhood: the gentleness that cared
Thus for a Child's small need: the simple, calm,
Unhastened task, that in the very words
The telling takes, is strong with humanness,
And sure with peace, and must forever keep
Him ours, and say forever she is ours.
Only that. No word of great travail,
No word of pain, or fright, or ecstasy,
No strangeness. Only that. The quiet hands

Wrapped him up in swaddling clothes, and laid him in a manger.

Her first gift then to Him, and His first witness
To the ways of earth, the first of tribute,
And the gesture that began the long
Fulfillment was a simple care she brought
To Him, not as a creature comes to stoop,
But as a mother bends to love. We know

No more than this, and what exchange beyond
Lies gathered to the spaces of her heart
To turn forever there, inviolate.
O, did she fold the veil down with her hands,
And raise them over Him, like frail, white wings
Of prayer? And brush His brow in lightest touch?
And look beneath His eyes that opened then,
And for the first time *see,* and know that she
Was seen? O, this is why His birthplace holds
No more than emptiness, stripped bare and clean
Of all the proud pretension we might hang
For feeble fringes, fraudulent with stale
Dishonors. We can grant no purer gift
Than she, and we are helpless to provide
Him whiter tribute than is held in these
Pale hands that hovered over Him, and that
Which rose to meet Him from her eyes.

And then
She knelt and held Him close against her heart,
And in the midnight, adoration fused
With human love, and was not separate.

And very near, the man named Joseph came.
He was not tired now, nor worn, nor sad,
His step was gentle, and a lightness soared
Within him till the memory of angel
Voices heard in dreams was now a less
Remembrance for him than the sight of hands
That held a sleeping Child.

He was the first
To find her thus, the first of all the world.

And when her faint smile called for him to take
Him for a breathless moment, he was first
To know there is no other blessedness.

The beat of pulses and the hush of heart
Had made again a silence more intent
Within surrounding silence . . . drift of time . . .
Starlight moving imperceptibly. . . .

The crunch of steps and voices from the dark
Were faint at first, but then the sounds grew clear
And separate until he knew that in
The starlight somewhere many shadows fell.
Louder voices spoke more quickly now.
A single step, then others following.
And Joseph stirred in answer, rising up,
But hardly had he moved, when suddenly
The voices hushed and footsteps too were held.
A first dim figure, dark against the wall,
Then swiftly, others clustering to kneel
In tangled shadow, and he turned to her,
To find the same faint smile that he had seen
When first he came to look upon the Child.

Tall men were these, the shepherds come from flocks
And wearing sheephides with the dew still wet
Upon the wool, with gourds and staffs, and one
With torches in his hands, and there was that
Upon each face that he might recognize.
And he no longer feared.

No further movement,

Till the youngest, kneeling still, moved on

From out the rest, and when his eyes had marked
The swaddling bands, and lingered for a moment
At a place where He was laid, he looked
To her, and did not shrink at what he saw.
The full words spilled to her in eagerness.
Of quiet flocks, the brightness in the sky,
The fear, protesting disbelief, and then
The greater fear: the music that had sifted
Down, more fragile than the light of stars,
And from a distance out beyond the farthest
Star. The pierce of it, the sweetness drawn
In the long, clear caroling of silver sound,
The mingling of the bells and echoing,
The upswift choirs and surge and flight of wings:
"O, fear not . . . fear not." Joseph's mind was quick
To understand. "O, fear not, but behold."

I bring you tidings of great joy, that shall be to all the people: for this day is born to you a Saviour, who is Christ the Lord, in the city of David. And this shall be a sign unto you. You shall find the infant wrapped in swaddling clothes, and laid in a manger . . . Glory to God in the highest: and on earth peace to men of good will.

The murmurs of assent spread down the cave
And rumbled to the entrance in the deep
Response of men's low voices, and a new
Quick crowding to the Child that was not boldness,
Yet was free.

And still was here a woman
Wrapped in silence, and the words were closed
Within her spacious heart for pondering.

It was not strange. These songs were of design,
Just as His breathing, or the straw. Not strange
His cherubim be jubilant and sing
For Him across the coasts of time. She seemed
As one who hears what is already told.
Elizabeth and Zachary . . . and Joseph . . .
Now these men. His world was widening. . . .

She smiled again, and the light was radiant.
Her hands were raising Him that they might see.

VI

THE hours then that moved across her heart
Were not the soft, obliterating fall
Of moments sifting as a dust to blur
The edges of the first impress of joy,
But were reiterated stroke of deep
Incising that should ever cut more sharp
And clear, until the moment that would be
His last at Golgotha will hold the force
To summon pain so deep its only measure
Be the long awareness of the years.
The hours then that moved across her heart
Dulled not the first quick sweetness of the night's
Small cry, nor slowed in her the rise of fresh
Bestowal, nor the grant of new response,
But only gave assurance to her fears
And to her questionings, and brought the ease
Of old maternal ministry to be
With her, His adoration and His praise.

Until the dawn came, and she held His face
More near to hers, and pulled the soft veil down,
And afterward looked up to Joseph's face.
He came near then, and they must rise to leave
This ground, and she must stand and carry Him
Beyond the reach of silent stars, and find
The road again that led back past the inn
Whose door had closed, and past the other doors,
And live the first of days.

What happened then?
There *was* return. Our thoughts are slow to move
Beyond the manger and the night that held
Within its kindly shadows all the harsh
Design, the blunt, hewn timbers of this place,
But yet, there *was* a dawn, and light that spread
Out coldly, inhospitable with cold,
So much the mind could feel it, and could wish
Again for darkness, and a further pause
Before the chill of issues need be met,
And steps now resting for so brief a time,
Must move again. And if this were a day
More fair, new life within it now to stir
The old and sluggish courses of the veins,
If a new heart now were beating, and new eyes
Were wide to catch the spread of light, it came
Above the skies' thin eastern rim still coldly,
As it always came, and what was new
Or kinder in it now was only marked
Within the Will of Him Who stands beyond
All time, and in the heart of her who keeps
The least of time held close for pondering.

Was there some good grant of welcome made?
Was there word and smile of gratitude,
Or gladness, or of honor? Pity, then?
Was there more now than a town distracted
In its own concerns? And had the speech
Of shepherds waked a wonder that endured
So long as to survive a night's full span?
And make a way less harsh for them to walk?
What happened when the manger held no more
The clothed in swaddling bands?

The angel songs
Are lost again as they were hid before
They broke across the sky, and poverty
And the unpretentious reticence that falls
So surely on the poor have covered them.
And Joseph was a man who searched, as many
Men had searched before him, for a place
To give a woman, and the woman's Child.
And after him, along the narrow street,
She walked and felt men pass, and held Him close
When there was sudden noise, or crowding near,
And looked again, and turned Him to the light,
And watched the eyelids lift and marked His hand
That brushed across His face, and then the slow
Relaxing of His sleep. And hurried some
Her steps to close again the distance fallen
After Joseph's quick determined pace.

To come, somewhere, at last where they might stay.
Whose house had opened in a place for them?
What roof of Bethlehem was kind to her,
And is unknown, except that she has known?
Some gracious door that must have framed a silence
When she showed Him proudly to the women
Who were kind, and said soft things, and smiled.
And then she rested in the place they made,
She tasted food again, and bathed her hands,
Felt the fire's warmth, and was so wise
As to be silent of the midnight choirs,
Content in Joseph's silence, till the songs,
Or stars, or angel presences gave leave
To speak of Him, or came again themselves.
There was no more, and trend of interest

And speech returned to more importunate
And brisker circumstance, of laws, and crowds,
The unaccustomed trading in the crowds,
Until her entrance and the Child that came
With her had found no more than casual
Response, and this good corner in a house.

And in a little while, she knew again
A nightfall that was quieter, and somewhere
When the town was still again, she slept.
And in the dark, and breathing there, and small
Within her arms' warm circle, He was sleeping.
And there was no care, and no concern
For Him, and no protection or defence
Except the arms that held Him, and the time
That moved across her heart for sweet increase
And mounting of a mother's virgin love.

My soul doth magnify the Lord: . . . Because he hath regarded the humility of his handmaid.

The days were long thereafter, drawn to lengths
And utter lifetimes in the poignancy
Of small succeeding tasks her hands might do,
And in the tensile sweetness, close to pain,
Of briefest episodes that fell along
The lingered moments of her care for Him,
And in the deep, unflowing pause of joy
A glance might bring, and for no greater reason
Than, not having looked, she looked again
To where His fingers lay.

But days were swift,
And piled in retrospect too rapidly

For counting in her heart, and were as one
Brief day, until the tone and trend of talk
That Joseph made with brethren in the house
Of Israel, recalled to her that eight
Had passed: and there was speech of law and word
Of old tradition, and the ritual
That drew the drops of blood and signed their sons
Beneath the covenant of Abraham.

God's way with men had been to take men's way.

So Joseph came, and when he stooped to her
To take the Child, their eyes were questionless,
And in the instant deeps the moment's look
Had raised between them, there was understanding
That the Child was also Abraham's,
And if no word was theirs to say of Him
Of how much more He was than Abraham's,
They were content. And she might think again.

He hath received Israel his servant, being mindful of his mercy. As he spoke to our fathers, to Abraham and to his seed for ever.

She gave Him gladly, and whoever spoke
With her and with the men who went with Joseph
As he carried Him, had cause to know
There was not need for speech or for a choice
Of any name that should be given Him,
Since somehow in the past agreement made
Had been remembered, and it was so strong
It left to them no further use in words.

And then return, and rituals were done,
And there was quick rejoicing and a kind
Word said for joy at simple faithfulness
To Israel that marked this house and gave
A new acceptance and obedience.
But in what stir of reverent gaiety
The flurry of the women's gestures made
About her, there was quietness on her
And a swift, sweet moment only Joseph saw.
He'd dreamed of it since first God let him dream,
And she had turned it in her mind and watched
Ahead with him to when it would be more
Than soft, respoken gladness in her thoughts.
No great display, and no significance
Observable beyond their deeper sight,
A moment only, hardly seen or heard,
Except he knew.

He gave the Child to her,
And she reached up for Him, and dropped her eyes
To close away surrounding presences,
And find the fairness of a white, white brow.
Only that he saw. A woman bent
In silence, with a wakened Child, and thoughts
That did not stray beyond the Child.

And then
He heard a single word she spoke within
The silence, and the sound her voice made, breathed
To him beyond the dearest hope of earth.
She spoke, and Joseph did not lose the sound
To memory. He heard her say but once:
"Jesus."

Then she folded Him again.
And when her eyes had lifted up, the moment
That had been, was gone. She smiled to him.
But he did not forget. For he had heard.
He told himself again . . . that he had heard . . .
His *Name!*

VII

THERE is no place upon the earth to stand
And be alone. And there is no retreat
That's deep enough to cut away the long
Claims of the past and sever ancestry,
To leave a clear and utter isolation
Where inheritance of modes and blood
And press of old decisions may not reach.
And if there were such place, it was not here
In Israel. The past here was more present
Than the day still trembling fresh from sunrise,
And the ancient sadness brooded still
Among the shawls and scrolls and chanted song,
And rising up from out the crusted years,
The sternness of a word as old as dust
Had hardened to a mold about her ways,
And set the course of them within a frame
That was not questioned.

No need for planning then,
Or thought of what might best be done, or what
Decision might include for her the most
Of wisdom. There was little to be said
Or done that any plan could alter much,
And what was looked to was not tentative,
Nor held for such by any who might see
The choice she made. The law was certainty,
And left decision purposeless and marked

Her for seclusion, and a little space
Her own until some forty days had passed
For purifying in the law's decree.
And since no sign or protest came of Him
Who gave the Child, nor word of stainlessness
That was the one clear breach within the web
Of common flesh, and single disavowal
In the earth's old stain, nor voices loud
Before the sun to speak exception here,
It was enough to bring the quick agreement
From her heart, and quiet acquiescence
To her days.

And she was grateful then,
That for this little while there was no more
Than time, and no more to be asked of her
Than loneliness with Him, and if the law
Came certain from the deep, remembered past
With lesser consequence than this, it earned
Good favor for the sudden wall it set
For her, to give again what Joseph gave,
And what the house of Zachary had held.

There will not be too much of griefless joy
That she might know, nor will there be too great
A space for her that holds not shadows falling,
Or the wait for shadows. And the long
Preparing loneliness that comes at last
Upon our hearts, close woven in the threads
Of human loves, will cover her too quickly
For much joyousness, and will be worn
Too young, and much too surely for her not
To feel the fall of it before it falls.

But now, there was the law. And for the glad
Duration of its span, no more than this,
That she would be alone with Him. And lost
To further venture in the care that need
Not seek beyond His cry, nor be concerned
With what lay past the measure of His want.
O, looking backward now, we only see
The law, and the end of it that Luke observes
When they had journeyed to Jerusalem,
But in between and hidden in the words,
Wedged in between the phrases, are the days
That were her own. Young days! Joyous! Glad!
With laughter in them that was gayer prayer,
And rose so softly in the liquid sound
Of innocence that dared a sudden mischief,
Or a clear delight that He should wrinkle
So His brow! O, here was caroling
And song to ripple down the silver choirs
Infectiously, and stir the winged far edges
For a new and sudden flurrying.
These days were hers, as further days would not
Be hers, unsigned of sorrow, with a young
Maturity that cuts away the terms
Of wisdom to the deep simplicities
Of a heart that loves, and a Child to take the love.
Long days they were. She watched reluctantly,
To count the dawns and sunsets, joyous yet
In the wealth of them that still remained. To kneel.
To breathe across the fairness of His hair.
To watch His eyes unfold. To know their search
For her, and in the joy of it, to close
Her hand impulsively upon the hand

That Joseph gave. To lift dreams out of dreams
And hold them real.

O, He Who gave the Child
Will ask for much, but this good space God gave
For her to keep, and set a law that she
Might know no harsher thing than lullaby,
And find no darker venture than her prayers.

And after the days of her purification according to the law of Moses were accomplished, they carried him to Jerusalem, to present him to the Lord.

This is a stained glass episode, filled in
With bloodless portraiture, and set with bleak
Formality, with cushions banked to stiff
Straight lilies, and antagonistic splendor
Flattened in its vague, uneasy gowns.
Except it was not so. And she was still
A woman, dusty for the six mile road
With a Child that pressed her warm beneath the shawls,
And with a heart that wished no more than this,
And what discharge or burden or demand
Would come of it, and what humility
Until the word to speak beyond the silence
Be another word than hers.

The gates
Of hammered brass were burnished to the sun,
And broke the Temple wall for gorgeous entrance
To the spacious courts and terraces
That were the honor of her fathers' race,

And pride of Israel. And when the tall
Reflections swung not far within the light
Of morning, she had come to them and stood
Here while her eyes swept up the great, high walls
And caught the rising smokes of sacrifice
That curled and twisted for a burning sign
That Israel still held the thousand years
Of covenant, and had not smothered yet
The fires of tribute, nor the pleading hopes
That were the world's hopes, and the pulse of dreams.

But then her glance returned to Him Who was
Her Child, and for a longer moment now
Had rested there, and marked there was no sign
In Him save quiet breath, nor other vesture
Than the blue cloak folded over Him.

Joseph's gentle touch broke in to ask
An end of thinking, and a step or two
Of hushed advance had brought her in to him,
Until the sandals that had rested once
Within a manger place, were treading now
So softly, softly, down the courts of God.

He gave her then the gray form of a dove
To hold, and first of two that she might bring.
Her fingers closed on it, and for a little,
There was some confusion till the shimmer
Of her shy smile and an upward look
Made Joseph take the Child, and give again
His poor gift of a dove, and she could go
To where some women were preceding her,
And the tall priest made the stroke of sacrifice.

It had been always so when quiet moments
Made a space when he might look on her.
When she had paused once in the fragrant dusk
Of Nazareth and leaned against the frame
A door had made, when he had come upon
Her, distant in a prayer's forgetfulness,
When she had knelt to stir a fire, and when
Her brow was creased and knit for trying so,
He'd known then all the surge and beat his cryless
Love made deep within him, and the break
Of it about her head, and what its strength
Was, veined within his days, yet looking now,
The poignancy and breast of it was more
Than what he'd known. So fragile there she was.
So eager in a secret innocence,
So lost among the rest who came to give
Such sacrifice as stain and stain's transmission
In the cord of life had asked. Whose Child,
Whose Child . . .

But then his thoughts were stopped again
In what he saw. A bent, submissive head,
And white hands lifting up a young dove's warmth
To other hands that did not pause to take
This gift she made. Her gift, *her* gift, of sin!

His arms closed tighter on the resting Child,
And muteness strengthened on his lips in old
Stern sanctity. But there was nothing else
To mark this gift, nor any signature
To say it was not made as others' gifts.
And then the white hands held the second dove,
Again content to close upon this least

Of sacrifice the law could countenance,
And asked no more, since poverty could bring
No blemish, but could only burn itself
More total gift. This was for gratitude.
For praise. For holocaust and sign of praise.
For fruitfulness and life and cry of life.
A sacrifice to gather up in one
Redemption all the locked, deep, turning cries
And plea of new maternity to give
Them utter speech and ease the wordless breast
Its inarticulate and aching praise,
But hallowed now, and for this whiter instance,
Clear and lustered in an undismissed
And blessed virginity, and made of her
Whose heart could know what Majesty had stirred
To life beneath it, and how much of need
There was for gratitude. She raised the gift
In movement of surrender, and the fires
That burned in immemorial sacrifice
Upon the altars of her race, flamed up
Again, and Israel renewed its sign
Of tribute for a male Child that was born.

What nameless priest was witness to this flame?
Who watched and marked the tears and bended head?
Who saw the lifted hands and took the gift
For Bethlehem? And heard what prayers were said
That were the first to rise of all the earth
To break in liturgy across Jehovah's
Courts and speak our gratefulness for us?

But if his name were known, what sight he had
Was only of a worn and fringeless shawl,

And upstretched hands refolded now in prayer,
Unless he saw her eyes, and marked the look
Of distance in them, when his mind might find
Some drawing towards her, and a lighter peace
Surrounding him than any he had thought
Was possible, and for an instant, guess
That he was witness and a minister
For greater holocaust than what he knew.
It was not spoken or betrayed by any
Least of sign, and was not made of doves,
Or fires, or any gift that might be grasped
Within a hand's embrace, nor was it new
With her, but was a fire that flamed again
Behind her eyes, and burned among the ashes
Of her total heart, and gave again
A gift that she had once made utterly.

Be it done to me according to thy word.

Then Joseph came to her and with the Child
Again she moved across the broader court
And down the great, wide spaces toward the steps
That now were free to her. She might ascend
Them now, and stand within the square high door,
And at another court could offer Him,
The First Born, to the service of the Lord.
And in release of it, her pace was queenly,
And a dignity that was not pride,
Nor conscious that it shone in humbleness,
Attended her. This was the house of God.
Her house. Her race had builded it and kept
The memories and vigils in these halls.
The sound of prophecy and roll of psalm

Had echoed here, and here was certainty,
And an old loved place that she might take and know
Of all the earth where might be found good peace.
And Joseph could not feel he was alone.
He sensed the sanctions here that were around
Her, and the strengths that would be raised for her
Beyond his own poor strength: and then he judged
The few coins that he held for ritual
Of ransom would be well received, and serve
The Temple's tribute, and secure for Him
An honored freedom. And for her, the Child.

They must have stopped before the mounting steps
Set circular athwart the pavement's end,
To gather up the sum of all events
Hid deep in them to bring this moment's fall:
The voices speaking and the dreams, His cry
Within the midnight, and the feel of Him,
The shepherds' faces and their kneeling forms. . . .

He shall be great, and shall be called the Son of the most High, and the Lord God shall give unto him the throne of David his father: and he shall reign in the house of Jacob for ever.

Then steadily, the Child held close to her,
They moved on upward toward the vested priest
Awaiting them. A step and then one more.
Her prayers were mounting and an exaltation
Beat across the quiet borders kept
Secure within her strong and secret heart.
A step and then another, and the hands
Of Israel were reaching out for Him.

A word, and brief response, and then her eyes
Were following the gestures and the signs
Made over Him. And He was lifted up.
For dedication. High! For Israel!
Before the courts. Before the altars. High!
High! Within the house her fathers made.

The bright coins fell from Joseph's opened hand,
And her arms accepted Him again.

They turned.
There was no more. Except a joyousness
The veils could hide, and slow descending steps
That led down past the others gathered there,
And she was one of many who returned
To quiet cradles and the place a woman
Makes for watching. And no more of honor
Trailed across her quick, forgotten way
Than what was soundless in the fall of Joseph's
Steps and in the Child held close to her.

Until an old man's hand was hesitant
Upon the veils, and pale eyes looked to her,
Not boldly, but to ask a moment's wait,
As one whose inner mind knew certainty,
But held abrupt avowal from his eyes.
She saw his eyes, so luminous and teared
With such a seeking she had seen once strong
Beneath the eyes a shepherd boy had raised.
And there was understanding and an instant
Answer that should ask no further speech
Than what her heart heard, nor a greater need
Than that his eyes should ask to see. She reached

To him, and from her young arms Simeon
Received the Child, and for the space of more
Than all his lifetime held to Him, and lived
His lifetime to the utter ebb of it.

And when his white head raised, he spoke new words
For her to keep besides the shepherds' words.

Now thou dost dismiss thy servant, O Lord, according to thy word in peace. Because my eyes have seen thy salvation, which thou hast prepared before the face of all peoples: A light to the revelation of the gentiles and the glory of thy people Israel.

She knew. She knew. The soaring and the pulse
That broke to song and could not come to speech
Except in song. She knew this flame that burns
And flares until there is no light beyond
The light, nor anything except the white
Peace held in it, nor more intent, nor more
Desire . . .

But in his eyes, sobriety,
And a slow, expanding depth that looked to her
From out some darker knowledge that had come,
And a rise of tenderness that sank again
Before it lived long in the deeper tides,
Or was so bright she might be sure of it.
He gave the Child to her and in his lifted
Hand of blessing, there was that which almost
Spoke of pity, and a sad farewell.

She saw it then. And Joseph moved more near.
Her hands unconsciously drew close the veils
To hold the Child more firmly to her breast.

Behold this child is set for the fall, and for the resurrection of many in Israel, and for a sign which shall be contradicted.

Some darker knowledge that had come to him,
So firm now on the voice of prophecy.

And thy own soul a sword shall pierce, that out of many hearts thoughts may be revealed.

These words were said to her. There was no doubt
Of that, nor doubt that she had heard them said,
Nor circumstance, nor favor that could force
Them otherwise, nor change the sound of them.
And a strong unyielding steadiness that held
Beneath his eyes was graver than the words,
And said again they should not be unsaid.

Behold this child is set for the fall . . . of many in Israel, and for a sign that shall be contradicted. And thy own soul a sword . . .

These were for her, and moved behind the quick
Unlearned defences of her mind to strike
Them down and level them before the rush
Of changeless things that were no longer fears,
So distant they might be forever distant,

But were presences so hard and stark
That they could end for her her Bethlehem,
And break the walls that had been building since
The Child first reached to her. These were the throats
Of old and unforgotten prophecy
To cry again the dark pain of Isaias,
Lost awhile beneath the clearer joys
The Child fulfilled. And in the silence come
When last words blistered to the end of sound,
She knew what searing and what edge of fire
Had lain across her own word spoken once
For total gift: "O, be it done to me."

And listening, she pressed to her the Child,
Warm with her own blood beating in His veins,
With trace and molding of her face in His,
And with the brow that was her brow, and sought
Unerringly the sleep upon her breast.
And heard, and heard above His breathing now,
The long cry baying to the street, the beat
Of hammers, and the sobs that gasped the air
In torturedly, the dull sound of a thud
That wood should make, the cries, the wilder cries,
The laughter and the hiss of spitted lips,
And faintly, faintly, words that seemed to fall
From dark, unmeasured heights to shatter her . . .
The last sound of His voice that called to death!

There is no utterance or sign that Luke
Might leave for us among her garnered words.
Simeon could see no sign, except
The glance that may have fallen presently,
And in a long look, bound the Child to her.

It is not right to think she gave consent.
The break her heart made was a wider wound.
She held Him close: and with Him, willed His death!

And Joseph heard. He was standing there
And heard too plainly what the words had said.
They fell across his mind and raised a welt
That is not often marked, but which he let
Remain there secretly. These words. These words
That lashed at her and struck the innocence
That had been singing, and whose least song gathered
More for him than what he'd thought lay hid
Beneath the ache of unheard harmonies.
The pierce of sorrow and the bruise that came
So calmly, so relentlessly to her.
He knew them, aye, he knew them, and he saw
The pause, and followed down the glance that met
The Child, and saw so clearly and so deeply,
He was blinded in the pain of it.
But neither in his voice, nor in his touch
Was sign more obvious than what she knew
Was there. And wordlessly, he guided her
Beyond this place, and Simeon could watch
Them walking toward the gates of hammered brass
That broke the Temple wall for gorgeous entrance
Burnished to the sun.

There was a widow
Near whose name was Anna, and whose prayer
And virtue earned for her some good repute
Among the people, and who was not poor
Nor unrewarded at another Court
Than this. And she had seen them passing then,

And raised an echo in her voice of what
Had been observed, and followed them in trailing
Words and last escort of spoken praise.

And if she watched until the road had taken
Them again, she saw more than a child
Who held a Child, and in her prayer, she might
Have known,

This was a woman, wrapped in silence,
And the ache of silence was her heart
That tried to give all that it held to give,
And ever more.

VIII

JOSEPH knew the road then was the same
As they had walked up to Jerusalem,
Except that shadows fell across it now,
And on the road the morning's innocence
Had wearied and had thickened to a tone
Of worn experience that sounded less
Of hope and more of men's content to search
Some place of rest, and yet he knew the road
Was not the same, and there would be no roads
That were the same. An old man's utterance
Had fallen and there were no roads except
To lead to what he'd said, and no retreat
That held not echo and remembered sound,
And now the dull ache and the certainty
That yet were new, would grow until the pain
Was old, but not so old it would be less
Of pain.

This was the first for her, the first
Of longer roads that held a weariness
That set a slower measure to her steps
To drag them in fatigue. They did not speak,
And he could find no heart to search for speech,
But only walked with her, and let her find
His presence dimly in the thoughts that turned
Slowly as the road turned, and could hope
She found some warmer ease because he still
Was walking here, and if his pain were other

Than her own, since in it there was anguish
That she would be anguished, it was like
To hers in that it held no smothered cry
To lift against the thrust of it in her.
This was his own, that he could not recall,
Nor turn, nor break the weighted force of it,
Nor dull the jagged edge for her, nor take
Himself the unwithdrawn and chosen sword.
And would not wish to. Aye, aye, that was it.
He could not wish to! This was more, much more
Than once he would have judged a cherished hope,
And he would not have said it kindly then.
But it was so. And in the peace that came
When once he'd learned it from her own acceptance,
He had found that there are stronger ways
For love to build than in upthrown defence,
And deeper peace that is not strange to pain.

So new these words of Him that were of loss.
So fresh the stroke and cut and wound of them
Upripped across her mind and gaped and torn
Along her staggered, unrecovered heart.
So new refusal, so unlearned the sign
That said rejection, and the crossed intent . . .
She had not risen to more certain movement
Other than instinctive press and hold
Of Him, and closer folding in her arms.
That was all she knew of calm or ease,
And that was all procedure that her mind
Could reach to or could find. Now only this,
The long, unthinking grasp and hold of Him!
The consciousness. The feel and summoning
Of nearer Presence. And the need. The need!

That, and strong withholding of such cry
As might have broken from her trembling lips,
And stumbled this too stern and resolute
Direction of her steps, and been received
By him who walked with her in not too far
An understanding of what newer deeps
Had moved beneath her silence. And the pain
That turned and turned again, until the words
That brought it seemed a boundary the earth
Had, and there was no space or time that went
Before them, nor remembrance of a time
When she was younger and another self
Who knew but songs that sang a young girl's dream.
They did not speak, and there was none along
The shrill preoccupation of the road
To mark their reticence as more than patient
Seeking of a distant roof, and silent
Understanding of a common way.

They may have rested then where there was shade,
And water running, and the cool relief
It gave raised up some intimate and quiet
Words she murmured of the Child, and shared
With him, and they could smile again the brave
And dearer knowledge that He was a Child.

Simeon had pushed away horizons.
All the hurt and dull relentlessness
Of what he'd later said could not conceal
The breadth of them for long beneath the pain,
And she remembered now the majesty
His words intoned. The sound and sweep of them
That flung past Israel to wider skies

Than she had seen, that broke the boundaries
Of tribe and blood and took the broader earth
For province, and were heavy with the weight
Of taller crowns than Israel could give,
And ponderous in dim suggested portent
Of allegiances and loyalties,
So strong and far, the longest tip of shadow
From the Temple wall could only touch
The nearer edge and slender fringe of them.
The air turned sultry with the feel of it,
And she could sense a Providence and Plan
That moved beyond her down the stars and worlds
Inscrutably to seek its own design,
And find accomplishment beyond the space
Her arms made, and across her shattered heart.
She looked at Him again. And in the tears
That rose but did not fall, she saw again
No more than this sweet Child her songs had touched,
Yet so much more she knew He was a Child
Who answered to another claim than hers.

Simeon had pushed away horizons,
Cleared the earth and struck the veil of days,
And if this vision had not known full dark
Or all concealment in her wiser heart,
And had been glimpsed before if only dimly,
Now the breadth, the brightness and the width
Of it were certain, and could never fade
Again, nor for a moment be unseen.

And she could come with slower, tired step
To Bethlehem. And in a newer way
Say that the day was long . . . and she was quite

Fatigued . . . and had been at the Temple gates
But was returned for now.

* * * *

A star was in this night, and rising hope,
And haste to meet the hope, and eager feet
That found a last road in a longer search,
And moving to the star, were clear again
Of deference and all delay that asked
A question in a king's court for a King.
The Magi came of distances to find
This land, and bore with them the cumulus
Of all the wide and common expectations
Stirring vaguely in the secret thoughts
Of half the world, and in this centred place,
They spoke out bluntly and had asked to hear
An answer simple as the star. And were
Dismayed there could be now a lethargy,
And in this land no mounted crest of joy
About to break more strongly than their own.

Yet saw the long scrolls opened and a name
Pronounced reluctantly: "At Bethlehem."

And here more eager in this night, behind
Them left unheeded, cold responding fears
Their question raised, and did not know the plans
That creaked across the shuttered corridors,
And moved behind the windows shut against
The night and starlight gleaming in the night.

She did not see the star nor look to see,
And did not know that there was caravan
To follow on the road that she had walked,
Nor thought much of the road, nor of the night,
Except there was a lighted place for her
And a Child to hold, and not much further need
Of roads, but only need of quietness
And a slow, sweet space of sleep for her to guard.

Outside the vague sounds distant in the dark
Were less familiar but remained so distant
Only quick brief straying of a glance
Betrayed in her a slight attention drawn
A moment from the covered Child. Until
The distance suddenly was narrowed down
And sounds became so clear and numerous,
Her wide look sought for Joseph's face, and held
Him, and her breath was caught for listening.
The soft pad of assembling feet, the hushed
Commands, the unmistakable and patterned
Sound of men dismounting. Creak and ring
Of gear, assurances to labored beasts,
A shout, and then the hushing of the shout.
The whispers following, and then the silence,
And the faint, more steady sound of men
Approaching, and the knock that came upon
The bolted door, not loudly, nor too bold.

Joseph quickly noted how her look
Had lost what first concern and questioning
Were there, and saw in her what he had seen
Once in another night, and he was sure

Her heart heard searching, and some deeper need
That sounded here, and asked an open door.

And entering into the house, they found the child with Mary his mother.

We've made of this too long a tissued scene
Where printed camels stand for silhouettes
Against a pleasant sky, and gilded kings
Are poised and picturesque. And these have almost
Wrest from us the bold, barbaric splendor
Of the night and what the startled lanes
Of Bethlehem were witness to. We must
Not now forget the strangeness, and this one
Brief breach of poverty in all her quiet
Days, when she was rich, and suddenly
The Child was rich. Treasures of the East
Are here. Magnificence. And corded gowns.
And somehow we have sensed a variance
In the warm simplicity surrounding her,
And feel the native meanness of the gold,
And slower tears well up for this than come
Of shepherds looking to a broken stall.

But what of her who saw them in the door,
And watched the slow advance and spoke no word,
But only listened to the sound their feet
Were making and could feel the stroke her heart
Beat stronger to the wrapped and sleeping Child?
Her fair eyes widened that had seen so much
Of angels and so little of the earth?
She found them strange? The bearded, swarthy face

Of them, the foreign robes? Or was there here
A quick and deep inclusion and a bond
Made intimate and warm when once she saw
Within their eyes the one thing shining out
That for her was not strange? The written lines
Of Matthew are as brief as Luke's, and colder,
Save the chance phrase that he drops to speak
What bond there was. And when they fell upon
Their knees and set their hands along the floor,
Her heart cried to their hearts, and knew how poor
They were, and generous, made Him a gift
To them, before the casque of gold was raised,
Or frankincense was set beside the myrrh.

That was all. And she was older then
Than they, and gave permissions, and the shy
Consent that let them look on Him, and spoke
About the midnight, and from out the slower
Wisdom of the long weeks' pondering,
And with the inner wounds of Simeon
For deeper mercy, let them touch His cheek,
And gravely gave Him to their asking arms.

O, they had known across the star's long way
Whom they had sought, and names upon Isaias'
Scrolls were bruited in the common speech,
And they had heard of them. "Counselor.
Prince of Peace. Father of the world
To come. God the mighty. Wonderful."
But not in these was heard what gentleness
They found, nor good heart's ease of threadbare shawls,
Nor gracious speech, nor pale and patient hands,
Nor dignity of her who was a queen.

And finding these, they made an eager court,
The first she knew, and on our earth, the last
Until the years shall cast some fishermen
About her, and the Fire be given them
For crowns. And then, respectfully, they told
Her of the star, and as the words fell, telling
Of the roads and of the hopes, they knew
A gentler gladness and a quiet grace,
Half laughter rising soundless, half release
For all the rigid edges that had bound
And chafed their souls in, and the wide relief
Of nearness and a breathing, breathing ease.

There have been some to say theirs was a bitter
Wisdom that could stoop to humbleness
When they had sought a king's house for a King,
But these were men who saw a star and went
To follow it, who heard a Name and cut
The ground away and could not sleep until
They found the Bearer of the Name, and these
Were men so simple they were unconfused
By simple things, and as the shepherds, found
No strangeness in His swaddling bands, nor wonder
That the Child should ask no more than her.

She smiled again, and the light was radiant,
And her hands were lifting Him that they might see.

Joseph watched the crowding and could see
Upon her face fatigue she would not say
Was there, and marked the villagers that clung
Beyond the doorway, and could sense a longer
Wakefulness than would be good for her

Unless he spoke, and to his own reluctance,
Asked for theirs and said a quiet word
About the night and of what need she had.

And in some moments, he could wave farewell
And bolt a door and turn again to her
To softly speak, not of departing kings,
But of the homely needs that come with morn.

And after they were departed, behold an Angel of the Lord appeared in sleep to Joseph, saying: Arise, and take the child and his mother, and fly into Egypt: and be there until I shall tell thee. For it will come to pass that Herod will seek the child to destroy him.

This was another darkness than the night
He'd wrapped about him some swift time ago
To sleep in, and he woke to it as one
Who had forgotten that it was the dark,
And stared against it blindingly, and willed
To see where there was naught for him to see!
He moved a little, and the caught breath eased
Within his throat, and then was held again
For sudden, taut alertness that could strain
And make an utter search to catch a least
Sound where there was no sound. A movement then,
Frightened, lithe, and padded with a guarded
Silence brought him quickly near to her,
And to the Child, and he could see again
The quietness that rested on their heads
And how her hand lay near to Him, and soft
With sleep, and like a white, unfolded gift,
Still touched the edges of His wrinkled robe,

And still reached out to Him. The moment now
Was timeless in the dark and he could not
Have said how deep it was or what a space
The night moved while it held, but only knew
His eyes closed, and the pain of gratefulness
Released the slow tears and was eased in prayers,
And that a poor man knelt within the dark.

But then the words he heard were rousing him,
And streaked in fire across his mind, and raced
Again across his dreams and scorched his heart
For flamed remembrance. "Fly. O, fly!" they said
Again as if the echoes of alarm
Had rounded all the far angelic hosts,
And spilled to earth this screamed and shrilling fear.

"Fly! Fly! Take the Child and fly!"
He'd heard it said. And had not failed to mark
The urgency and rushed relentless import
In the cry and unbelievably
The last, chaotic words he'd heard burned white
Against the startled darkness of his mind
In searing flame he felt of blasphemy.
To destroy Him. It was that they said!
To destroy Him! He that was a Babe
Who might have been the thunder for a darker
Sinai! Who had chosen Infancy
And hands that could not strike, and Who had been
Content with helplessness for panoply,
And sought the one throne that could not be feared.
Who had not come alone, but asked the arms
Of one so sweet to hold Him, and to be
With Him lest there be strangeness or a form

Men might not understand and might not love.
But there was no protesting or appeal
That he could make, and if this were His word,
He would not wish it otherwise, and then
Before his hand fell down to waken her
And brush the warm sleep from her face, he thought
How deeply he had learned this of her days,
And would not follow with his mind, his heart
That still could hear the night winds blowing coldly,
And the lonely sound they'd make along
A road.

The words were strange then that he spoke
Within the shadows and the first confusion
And the drag that sleep held still upon
Her senses made of them but words remembered
From a dream so worried and apart
From context and so twisted she could find
No meaning, and could only hear the deep
Tone of his earnestness and how he tried
For reason and for calm. "Arise. Arise,
We must be gone," was what he said, and said
Again, and in such voice he seemed to plead
Beneath the uttered speech for grasp and hold
In her of reawakened bond and common
Heart that had no need beyond itself
For explanations or a reasoned speech.
And if the burden of his whole intent
Were held, there was no further need of Him
To ask of her again what had been asked
Not in his words, but in the sound of words.
She knew his deep beseeching, and could give
The trust that had been only slowed for sleep,

And find an understanding that had not
Been lost, but only waited for his voice
To summon it. She turned then to the Child,
And for a moment, listened to His breath,
And made communion in a kiss upon
His brow, then tucked the robes about Him so,
And with the deftness of a woman's gestures,
Reached for shawls, and pinned them, and pushed back
Her hair, and gathered up the rest of small
Belongings in her hand.

Joseph marked
The first of movement and the mute response
Of folded robes and quick efficiency
That made a light, and saw her swift search dart
And glance about the room, and he was gone
About his own sure errands of the water
Bags, and strapping of the tethered beast,
And soothing it in low, familiar words,
And anxious casting to the sky for sign
Of storm.

And in a while, so pitifully
Brief, there was no more for them to do,
And no farewell to take beneath the dark
Closed isolation of the night, and now
A haste, so silent it was fugitive,
And fear that chilled her in the cold contagion
Of his furtiveness, and then a last
Quick smudging of the lamp to put away
From her in sudden shut denial all
Security and warmth she'd thought to hold
To for a moment more.

And they were three
Who wandered in the dark, and sought a road.

He moved across the narrow streets and down
The long path to the village edge, and bent
So hurriedly against the slower pace
The ass was keeping that she knew again
The fear that drove him and awaited more
Of words to tell of it. And hushed the Child
Whose sudden cry was sharp within the night,
And pierced to her so poignantly there were
No fears, nor roads, nor dark shapes on the roads,
But only One Who cried and turned to her.

She held Him closer then and stroked His head,
And summoned what instinctive comforting
In gesture and in soft maternal murmurs
She might bring to Him, and saw above
His hair, the wide dark reaches of the sky,
So roofless, and the road that twisted out
To such uncertainty, and felt the wind,
The threats of scudding clouds across the moon,
And broke a young prayer crying up through silence,
Not for whiteness on her heart, nor joy,
Nor gratitude, nor for the touch of angels
In her bended praise, but only now
A plea for strength against the emptiness
And aid against the ache of helpless hands.

Joseph spoke of angels that had come.
And in the little leisure of a slower
Step, put confidence within his voice
For her, and said it was a blessed dream.

And they were watched for, and must go because
It was as he had heard one other time
At their betrothal, and had known the same
Good clarity. Her silence then inquired
For more, and almost he'd succeeded then
To calm, and to an ease, and said it was
Of Herod that he'd dreamed, or had not dreamed
So much as heard within a dream. Herod,
Who was now the king. It was because
Of him they must be gone.

The night winds gave
A freshness that was clean and smelled of freedom.
Stars were cool before his lifted face.
He had walked on a little, and was sure
Again that there had been no faltering
Or tears behind him, and he wondered why
He'd feared there would be, and remembered now
The words of Simeon that had not torn
The deep acceptance that he still could feel
So flawless and unshattered in the night.
And so he dared what he had left unsaid:
They would destroy Him. Aye, *destroy* the Child!

There was no more thereafter, and the word
Of Him he'd spoken dropped within the darkness
Like a smooth stone fallen to the deep
Unflowing waters of a stirless pool.

She did not move, and did not fret the far
Hid plans of Providence for signs or reasons,
Nor lift up a search demanding more
Of utterance, but only kept the pain

Uncried within herself, and let it lie
For deeper worship and for oneness made
With Him Whose form was gathered to the pain.

The hollow sounding of the ass's hoofs
Told of a hidden passage in the night,
And over them there was a woman riding
Who remembered now the broken beams
And stalls and straw within a manger place
That she was leaving, and the little streets
And roofs that had been dear.

He spoke again,
And was a man who seemed to have arrived
At firm conclusions and was confident
That he might speak them and be heard with some
Assurance. Egypt. Egypt was a land.
A safe land. Out beyond the land that Herod
Held.

The wind was rising and a leaf
Blown up of distances was caught across
Her hair, and clouds were racing down the far
Pale pointings of the stars. Egypt. Egypt.
Where was Egypt? It was far away.
Out there in the darkness. She had heard
Men name it sometimes as a land so distant
It was but a name. She had not thought
Of Egypt when the warm sleep came to her
A while ago beneath a roof she had. . . .

The wind was rising, and the hollow sound
Of hurried hoofs told of a hidden passage
In the night.

IX

LET once the mind perceive the gorgeous premise
Of the God Child, and it will not rest
Contentedly at silence, but will search
For wonders and attending brilliancies
That seem demanded, and, not finding them,
Will spin them out alone to trim the speech
Of truth in gay and brighter circumstance
That runs beyond the silence to unfold
What might be found, but is not found.

The whole
Eternal page of her and of the Child
Has been a scandal in its briefer tale
Of unexpected things; and if we'd ever
Dreamed of her before her days, and knew
Not what the hunger was that turned in us
And made us dream, and spun mythologies
That curl and spiral out as mists above
The deep, unmeasured marshes of the past
To take some several shapes that seem to move
Like her, we'd only told in them of want,
And twisted prophecy and deeper ache
For her that stems of a long forgotten source
Beyond remembrance. And in all this need,
This vaguer yearning of our lonely blood,
We had not fashioned other than a shade
Of truth, nor cast of her more than a trace
Of valid molding or expectancy.

We're much too dark of mind, and much too small.
Our race knew not her stature, and she walks
Beyond us, other than our thought could frame.
We could not fancy *her,* nor guess her simple
Annals so. There's not enough of facile
Splendor and too much of homely things.
We'd guess the star, but who would guess the stall?
Who'd look for shepherds? Dream the swaddling bands?
And add for them a poverty so real
It is no different from the ancient hurts
That worry in the hearts of many men?
We'd not devise this Child Who falls in sleep
With no more liturgy than any child.
We'd give her honor and nobility,
Be tempted of a wide magnificence,
But whence the meekness and the wearied hands?
The quiet eyes? The *hiddenness* of her?
The pain? The pain? What dream included that?
Or thought the steady cold of loneliness?
The innocence? Or would have been content
To say so much, and then to say no more?
And leave an unanticipated silence
Calmly mute and set forever wordless
Where we would have hoped such weave of words?

That's not the way of fables but the way
Men speak when it is given them to speak.
And we have been impatient of such wisdom
And have chafed at Matthew and have made
Embroideries of further words to web
The silences he left with intricate
Detailing, and there are long sentences
Designed somewhere, to tell more of this lonely

Flight than loneliness, and more of her
Who raised the wakened Child and turned her steps
Beyond the roofs of Bethlehem and faced
The night winds on the southward moving road.

They're filled with hollow speaking and relate
The much too ready marvels of the birds
That fluttered down to hover over them
In winged escort. Of palms that bowed before
Her way with fruit. Of wolves couchant and bent
In awed submissive tribute, and the sands
That bloomed and sudden springs that gave clear waters
At the mark her feet made in the dust.
And we are certain that a small ambition
Fancied these, and in the multitude
Of wonders piled about her, catch the sound
Of discord and a noise that beats against
The undemanding reticence we've heard
Of her, and harshly breaks across the calm
Of her revealing and the silent, deep,
Uncluttered glory of her simple way.

(He) arose, and took the child and his mother, by night, and retired into Egypt: and he was there until the death of Herod.

And that is all. This meagre brace of words
That falls down like a rigid gate to shut
Away from us the fuller sight of heartbreak
And the lonely roads, and what it was
That lay between this too abrupt departure
And the long return. We'd ask for more.
We'd hope, and look into the hopefulness

For sight, and seek the turnings and the halts
Along the way, and ask to know the fears
That moved on her poor roofless vagrancy
And carried Him in secret like a shame.
We'd ask for more. But we must be content
With only this, and hunger, and the mind
Must wait upon the heart to reach beyond
The limit set within this ended speech.
These silences are many, these abrupt
Conclusions that can leave the thoughts to swing
Away in impetus to dizzy arcs
Of wide conjecture. One of them will hold
The length of Nazareth's unspoken years.
And one of them is here, this lesser silence
Of the outward road, that leaves her walking
On the road. We do not follow her.
The uninstructed mind can see no farther
Than a little desert dust that rises
Once and falls, and then is stirred again
In answer when a king has died. And if
We'd search beyond, we must not trust too much
The much too ardent mind, unless it stop
At what is told of her, and what the heart
Remembers of its own validities.

O, they were not the first from out the tribes
To tread this southward route with fear to drive
Them and to stab against their heels for goad.
This was the famine march, and Israel
Had hungered on it to the sheds of Egypt,
And an old flight marked this dust ahead
Of them with harried steps and made of it
The dry, recorded path to refuges

Beyond the border's edge. These arid hummocks
And the stubborn stalks along the road
Were not so kind to sight or memory
To give assurances to her and ease
The long anxiety that looked beyond
The next bare rising hill, and shaded Him
Against the sun's scorch and the sting of sand.
And this was not the road that led to home,
Or turned itself among the fields of home,
Where roofs and wells and graves and common accent
And allusion in the daily speech,
Where all regrets and hopes, and sobs and laughter,
All were held and hallowed in a single
Air and one tradition that had grown
So old it gave the worn security
Of what is old. This was an outward road,
And after it, her face was alien.

Behind them something brooded in a fear
That stirred the angels to a sudden cry.
Though it had been in dreams that Joseph heard,
The fear was now no dream, but breathed at them
In every wind that flowed across their throats.
They felt it following and keeping pace
With them. The vagueness of its threat was fear
Beyond the fear. It was a footstep heard
Within the night, a horseman passing them
Who came more swiftly down the northern way,
A word, a scrutiny, a clustered knot
Of men that held a few heads that had turned
When they had passed. It stopped with them, and lay
Along the ground beside their fitful rest,
And more than tiredness had drawn the thin

Lines to her eyes, and stretched the tight pain aching
In her brow; and then the words were good
That Joseph spoke, that said how small they were,
And how much space had fallen in their wake,
And that the word or sword or what was driving
Them was still behind them, and he'd learned
The road was not too barren, nor too distant
Now, and at another dusk they might
Expect an end of it.

And if she heard,
And found some faint abatement of the fears,
Or if she only heard, the deep kind rumble
Of his voice could give enough for her
To rest in, and unseen, she may have smiled
A little in a small half dreaming kiss
Upon the Child's fair hair, and in the soft
Caressing stroke her cheek touched to His brow,
Could dream for both their gratitude, and bless
The sturdy heart and feet that guarded them.

Joseph had not looked for prodigies,
Nor, more than she, had searched the skies for sight
Of pillared fire or cloud to be with them.
There was no quest among the dews for manna,
Nor for rocks to strike for unexpected
Springs. He'd heard a word of threat and flight,
And felt in it the draw upon his strength,
The sinewed drain and summons in the cry.
It burst within *his* mind, and called to *him*.
And he was not a man to wait for more
Than that. It was enough to bristle him

To utter spending, and to make him grasp
Within his hand, his wisdom, all his hard
Strength, lean from labor, what he had of goods,
And craft, and what he knew of prudences,
And bend them to a willed and fierce protection
He might throw around her and would hold
Against the wear of days, and prodigal
In more than stubborn honor to a trust,
Would keep until his last strength ebbed from him,
And till his last prayer died upon his heart.
And so he counted miles and found a way
That skirted unobtrusively in places
Swiftest and most secret, calculated
Shrewdly for a five night road, and watched
A pace that might be thought the best to fall
Between her eagerness and need for distance,
And her weariness. And he could know,
And in the tired silence of the march
When dust had streaked so dark beneath her temples
And the sun's glare stung behind her eyes,
She too could know again . . . He was a Child,
And for the durance of a Plan that made
Him so, would be no more than that, a Child
She held and ran away with in the one
Defence that lowliness can hope to wield,
And in the only safety that the poor
Can find. A Child, to lift, and nurse, and soothe,
And fan the flies from when the air was still,
Who called to her in only helpless cries,
And left her but a woman who must follow
Where a Child's needs led, and where a kind
And fumbling hand searched out a path for her.

The hours passing and the driven steps
Of exile led them deeper into strangeness
Till the very stones and plains and skies,
The sight of valleys and the names of hills,
The straggling faces meeting them, the words
Exchanged, the sound of voices, now could hold
The hard aloofness of unknown, unfriendly
Things, and when they'd stopped, and in the night time
That came down around the strangeness, made
The warm small circle of a fire's light,
And when he saw her eyes that followed him
And did not turn until he'd moved beyond
The light, he guessed of how much more he was
Than one who gathered sticks and spoke with her.
He knew he was a homeland for her heart,
A wide, wide acre where she was not strange.

And he was glad, and grateful for the dreams
That made it so and placed him here, and felt
The stronger surge within him of an old
Humility that his could be the name
And strength that held the fears off and surrounded
Her, and that in what he was and what
He knew, there was enough to build for her
This roofless refuge, and enough to give
Her hungry prayers to freedom, and to grant
Some sanctuary for her virgin praise.

She had not lost the clear awareness made
Of conscious limits that His Presence set
For her, and if there were some fears, and days
That rushed in fugitive and frantic haste,
A sword that swung behind her driving her

Across the gates of Israel because
She held a Child, and sending her as Eve
Was sent, to darkness and to ways that are
Not fair, and if the sun died red along
A far horizon, menacing, and shapes
Were strange, and out beyond the hills a wilder
Strangeness waited, still upon her heart
Was quietness, and in the dark, the deep
Unshattered poise and consciousness yet held
The silver flame of her to burn for Him.
So steadily. Unfaltered by the smokes
Of sorrow. Clear. It burned here in the night.
Unseen beyond the ranks of hiding angels,
Unperceived and tall within the dark.
The silver flame of her about His head!
That touched Him, and could keep within the vast
Unheeding sweeps of distances and stars,
The pure and stainless essence of the one
Untarnished, undiminished flame of praise
That ever will rise up for Him.

This was
A woman wrapped in silence: and the shrine
Her thoughts made gathered her beyond her exile
And enclosed a native place where all
She loved could cancel banishment, and hold
The votive pleading of her single prayer
That asked to be only in that place
Where He will be.

The ground of Egypt eased
The urgency of fear that had been pressed
Around them since the broken sleep, and once

They felt it grind beneath their feet, the pace
Was slowed, and they could breathe and lean against
Its broad security, and lift their heads
And know a freedom where the only pain
Was loneliness and that they were not free
Except in loneliness. And for some moments
They had been content to do no more
Than walk more leisurely and taste the sad
New joy of sudden ease, and find how much
Of weariness had come, to be a promise
Now of rest, and long and grateful time
For dreamless sleep. And here, it seemed to them,
The distance of the days since first she stepped
Across the Temple stones to hear the hard
Word that had broken innocence and struck
Her song, was greater even than the length
Of wastes that stretched behind her to the place
Of Bethlehem. So many lifetimes now
Had fallen, and the scars were cut so deep
Within her heart that she could stand as one
Too quickly grown, and wise in old remembered
Patiences, could look across to find
A day no more remote than yesterday
Was far from her as childhood, and as dear.
And when the wearied airs of Egypt parted
To receive her and the first fresh sweetness
Of the blowing veils, the newer fragrance
Spread to them, the lifting life that ran
Like sudden impulse for a clearer Spring,
Were taken of a sorrow, and were old.

They had no dreamed, anticipated place
Of refuge they might ask for in a name

More clear and definite than any other
Name. And there were here no friends to seek,
Or threshold that could now be guessed more warm
And friendly since their feet had wandered up
And waited, homelessly. It was to Egypt
They had fled, and now that this was Egypt,
That was all, and one poor place or town,
Or one odd road or several kept as much
For them of hope or preference or promise
As the rest could hold, and where they stopped,
Or what direction now they judged was best,
Could not be thought to seize an interest
That weighed much, or was felt beyond their own
Poor worried need, and on the road they watched
The surer tread of swift complacency
That passed them and contained its own rebuke
Against their hesitance, and gave to them
A cold assurance for the inner doubts
Of worth that unprotesting stirred in them.
He was not suave of speech, or confident
In conscious wealth that might be used against
An easy disrespect. He had not traveled
Much, and only had sincerity
And deeper unenameled honestness
To bring with him across the kinder limits
Of his fathers' ways. And there was need
In him of other talents than the eager
Strength that sought the road and raised defence
Against the simpler threats of breaking thunders
And the rains. This was a foreign land.
They were accented strangers seeking here
Who must now ask against indifference,
And break hostility, and find among

The sparse, contested pittances of foreign
Crafts enough of substance to withhold
The edge of hunger and secure some place
Against the need of quietness, and there
Was on him then the strong, unspoken pledge
His heart made that whatever place, or town,
Or roof, or unpretentious wall should close
About her, it should not be left too harsh,
Nor for her gentle aristocracy,
Unkind.

It is not too absurd to think
They paused a little off the road and gravely
Spoke together, and decided plans
And pieced opinions, and compared the hopes
That might be met, and he was not aloof,
Nor too reserved, nor too severely set
In independence to inquire of her
Her woman's word, and in the low speech spoken,
An accord returned, and in the slow
Warm rise of wistful gaiety, exchanged
The gift of confidence, and they were strong
In other sureness than the lifted prayers.
And in her arms, the Child again was sleeping,
And the issue of their quiet words
Was all the wisdom that would mark for Him
What path He'd bless, and what poor barren folk
Would look upon Him, and would never know.

Many places now have claimed to keep
A memory of them. They may have been
In all or none, and traces now are hid
As was the purpose and intent they should

Be hid, and we can only guess that they
Had chosen some place where the tribes had flung
A broken fragment, and their own were near.
And that they lived a while in this or that
Sad colony of Israel that spotted
This too old land of the river's gift,
And made a place of exile and of tears.
He knew the need of some quick price or market
For his strength, a place to sell himself
And scrape out with his skilled and patient hands,
A lean frugality for her, and knew
Her greater need that old familiar words
Could ease, and men might give who spoke in psalms,
And had been warmed at memories and hopes.
And he remembered too, and spoke with her
For comfort of the long return, and strayed
Not deep within the strangeness, that the word
That was to come, or glad command that sometime
Was to fall to waken them again,
Would find them near.

And Egypt closed on her
Like some enveloping and scarlet mist
To take from us behind the swirling scarves
The small clear figure of the silvered grace
Who walks within so sweetly with the Child.
This is a land of flood and spawning mud
That steams in the lush growth of the seeding grain,
Of hates and cruelties and slaves, and thick
Gigantic gods, impassive in the stone.
Of fears, and reedy pipes that whine among
The dead, where sparrowhawks and stiffened eagles
Spread against the gold sarcophagi.

And for a little while, she walked on it,
And trailed across the dense and unresponsive
Darkness with the Light, and was the lost
And unsuspected bearer of the Light.

We do not see her movements nor the places
That her feet touched in the little tread
Of crystal innocence, and cannot know
The hiding sanctuaries of her rest.
And Egypt did not know, nor felt the throb
Of lifting lightness that could run from out
The shining Halo at her breast to thrill
The staled air of the sated plains to whiter
Dreams and quick uprising hopefulness.
But she had known. And could have told the pain
Of all the slow miles drawn through her, and said
How deep the secret was that was His Name.
She knew, and in the long days let the darkness
Cover her, and kept the lonely watch
So silently, and with the Child that rested
In her arms, she waited for the word
To rise again and move across the dark
In good return. She saw the amulets
Of curling snakes, the scarabs and the crawling
Tribute ranked about the golden beast,
She heard the deep gongs sounding in the throat
Of Egypt for a sob, and marked the dull
Fears sunken in its eyes, and saw the beaten
Poor. And if the songs she wove and placed
About His head were taken of the old
Songs of her heart, they spoke again of pity,
And the peace that once was clean and bright
Upon the face of shepherds and the brows

Of kings. And when the sullen darkness crept
About Him and she was alone, and psalms
And pleas, and hopes of Israel were far
Beyond the darkness, and her heart was small
Against the press of loneliness and tears,
She held Him closer for a secret praise,
And waited, waited for a word of Him,
And in the waiting was not sad.

X

THERE is a way by shrewd comparison
Of kings' reigns and the shuffle of the crowns,
By scraps of names and interlocking eras
To compute, with only faint pretence
At guessing, what the length was of her days
In Egypt, and to say how long the pain
Endured between the slow recurring dawns
Of exile and its falling dusks, and in
The quiet patience of her hopes, looked out
So undemandingly to secret night
That would be lifted in the last of dawns.
But in whatever judgment we might form
Of weeks or months or dull revolving years,
We'd only find a word to speak of time,
And there are few in exile who remember
Time, but only waiting for the end
Of it, and neither of her lost, uprooted
Loneliness, or what remained undimmed
And undistracted in the loneliness,
Can sum be made, unless we find a name
To give unfallen tears, and some account
To tell the total of the soundless words
That moved unfaltered for serenity
Between her soul's uplifting and His claim.

Some space of prayer, of labor, and of wait,
A little while of strangeness, and the deep
Unflawed acceptance of the banished place

And what it held of distances and days
Or further days, if need be, and again
He heard the voice that sounded in his dreams.
It did not cry, but only whispered now
A milder speech of soft returned content.

Arise, and take the child and his mother, and go into the land of Israel. For they are dead who sought the life of the child.

This was more leisured journeying, more calm
For lack of fears, and preparation could
Be made, and gentleness could pause to speak
Farewells, and take the offered gift of kind
Good wishes, and accept such words as come
To them who leave an exile and begin
The road to home. There were no quick alarms
To harry them and mute their tightened lips
To all but meagre bitten speech of fear.
The skies were spacious now, and there was laughter
For the rain and little pleasantries
To make about a long day's tiredness,
And shy contented rest beneath the stars.
Clouds were things to watch and follow down
The skies, and made her hug impulsively
The Child for joy of them and for the white
Forms sailing; and the hills assumed some look
Or half detected look she might remark
To him of recognition, and the turns
The road made lifted eager sight to catch
A further turn, and sent her searching till
The narrow thread was lost along the distance,
And her eyes were gay with seeing it.

A youngness stirred in her and unrepressed,
Was glad for no profounder reason than
The heart's return to places of its long
Remembering. It moved in her and raised
About her, soft, more luminous and bright
Aureola to cover in the cast
Of whiter joy, the sterner constancy
And grave intentness of her mind, and was
As children's trebles running on the sound
Of prayer, or light, that unsubmissive, laughs
Within the faded eyes of innocence
Grown old.

To be returning. To have heard
Assurance and to know these eager steps
Were still obedience, and kept again
Fulfillment in their peace, as other steps
Had kept it in the pain. To find the ease
Of freedom. To unloose the mind and shake
The fears out that had creased so deep with time.
To feel the flow of kinder airs that were
Not hostile or afraid. A peace was here,
And calm that came about them in the rise
Of tranquil promise of a greater calm,
And in the slow repeating of the hoofs
The reveries were moved, and soothed content
Could let him think how round her voice had grown
For gladness, and it seemed to him the sound
Of it was newer song to tell of joy
Again across a new nativity,
And that from out the long dark, she had come
To bring the Child for Israel again,
And hoped for other shepherds gathering.

Joseph thought of Bethlehem, and marked
The good warmth that the name made in his mind.
To bring again the quiet stars and crib,
And all the long days that had held the first
Fresh wonder, and the peace that lay on them
As clear as light that reaches to the pale
Grey hush of dawn. He spoke of it to her,
And saw remembering that woke behind
Her eyes, and in a moment heard the words
She said to him in grave consideration
Of the Temple gates that would not be
Too far from Bethlehem and turned the slow
Revolving feasts and kept His mannered praise.
They might be often there from Bethlehem.
And this was David's city, and the kings
Had knelt there, and its fields had seen the light
Of angels. Aye, there was so much for them
That might be thought direction, she could add
Her own wish to his plans. And smiled assent.

He swung the path then, glad that he had found
All sanction, and he spoke with confidence
Among the small remarks exchanged at crossroads
And in places of an evening's pause
Of where they journeyed, and the hopes they had
Of reaching it, and made an easy mention
Of what town they sought. And heard within
The talk a word that scratched across his mind,
But faint at first, like some less easy sound,
Half noticed and persisting, till the wedge
Of it had grown and forced a wider break
Unwilling in his calm. It was a name
He heard respoken and perceived the lowered

Tone that went with it, and could not lose
The sound of ominous and reawakened
Fear it raised in those who spoke and those
Who heard. It was a king's name. Archelaus.
Archelaus. He who was the son
Of Herod and who stood within the room
Of Herod over Bethlehem, and held
The same fear that had died when Herod died.

His sleep then was a troubled thing again.
Or was not sleep but only seeming sleep
He held to that the fear that woke and moved
Above his thoughts be not observed, or break
The calm that rested on her own sweet sleep,
Nor strike the sword again until he'd come
To some decision of its weight, or was
More sure of all the portents, or at least,
If there could be no longer hiding, till
He'd found some reasoned word of peace to give
To her in balance for the word of fear.
He thought of how men looked, and what their accents
Were beneath their answers when he'd asked
The name the king had who was now the king.
He turned again the words and thought of flight,
And thought again there was no need of flight,
And twisted back to certainties he was
Not sure of, and accepted doubts for fears,
And fears for doubts, and suddenly he found
That he was listening.

And woke to hear
Again in memory of dreams a voice
That whispered of a quiet land to him

That he had known once and that she had known
And where there were no fears, but only peace.

And so the word he had to say to her
Was not a word he found reluctant, nor
Could wish to leave unsaid, nor one that called
Again the dark processions of concern
To walk across her mind, but only meant
A deeper quietness and more remote
Seclusion in the hills that had not seen
The stars and shepherds, nor had heard of kings,
Nor knew of Simeon or what had fallen
In the smokes about an altar's flame,
And was a little place of little homes
And ways that were the old ways of her race,
And undisturbed.

He said it must not be
To Bethlehem. There was a king who held
A harsh rule on the land of Bethlehem.
But not beyond. And they must go beyond.
It had been said to him. They must return
To Nazareth, to Nazareth.

The word
Fell softly, and she let it come among
The still things resting in her inner heart
Where there were only still things, and a few
Dear names, and some unaltered certainties.
It settled like a sound that had been always
Heard, or always waited, and had sought
But this one stronger utterance to fall
The full depth and be laid among the old

Things that are not relearned but only need
Awakening. It stirred again in her
The smell of fields and woods and winds and raised
The voices speaking that had not been answered
For so long a moment there was more
Than good release from exile on her tears.
It told of thresholds and the doors where she
Had laughed, and heard behind her in the good
Including sound of closure, and the gate
That she had walked to on a day for peace,
And found that Joseph made it so, and held
The peace secure beneath the uneventful
Turning of a village ways.

And when
The word had grown within their speech until
Acceptance held no longer edge of new
Decision, they could find what else it said
Than prudence and retreat before a new
King's hates, and came to wider calm that lay
Behind the word's first meaning and perceived
The deep intent.

This turning of their steps
From Bethlehem was sign this was an end
Of wings and signature of more than earth,
And was an end of stars. And gave the first
Sweet intimation of their longer ease,
And set the first low sighing of its breath.
To Nazareth. To Nazareth. It was
As if the voice upon the dreams had grown
Content at silence and had turned to whisper
In a last word of a dreamless rest.

Of how the long unfolding now would be
No more than falling days and only sweet
Unstraining flow of time. There had been much
Across her young years crying, and the break
Of it had riven to the inmost cores
Of ecstasy and struck to the ash dry cuts
Of fear. She had been ministered by angels,
Watched the first rise of the light beneath
His eyes. She'd heard the word fall of His pain,
And had been lost with Him. But only now
This calm path that was bringing her again
As one returning who had only gone
Across the valleys on a longer path
Than most, and had been lingering a while;
But come now, with a Child within her arms
To be at home again. There was no more
For her to hear than ease, and no more roads.
And if she knew the wound within her heart
Was only healing for the deeper stab
Of swords, and that there was another tryst
For her in loneliness, her eyes could fall
To find how small His hands were yet, and see
How still His brow must lean against her breast,
And that there was no dark appointed place
Of further tears, but only all the young
Days growing, and the homes of Nazareth.

XI

THERE is a way we have who walk the earth
Of finding somewhere on its wide too distant
Spaces, some good smaller ground or some
Few squares of ground that hold a boundary
The heart has drawn and set there for its own
Observance, and which keep behind the dear
Apportioned border more than all the earth,
And more than can be lost among the wayward
Years or left to be confused with wider
Memories. And she was of the earth.
And knew with us the common mold of it,
And if her feet have gone forever past
Our roads and past the pathways on our hills
To tread before us in a place we have
Not walked, and if the lingering of frail
Enduring fragrance, and the sound of prayers
And beads and hopes and songs and bravery
And some persuasive call to virtue now
Are all the sight we have of her, she still
Was of our earth, and has not lost the names
That are her own, and still must keep the sound
Of them reechoed to the earthless praise
In her eternity.

And one of these
Is Bethlehem. Where first the stars looked down
Unfaltered at Him first beneath her hands.
And one, another name, is Calvary.

The dark place of the pain and of the words
As edged as iron that came like falling shafts
Across the quivered hours until the last
Sound stopped within her offered heart as His
Broke in His blood. Aye. One is Calvary.
And one is nameless. Save as she recalls
The fragrance and coolness of the dew
And of the lilies where she waited Him,
And heard His risen voice, and raised her face
Beneath her greyed hair to the fresh winds moving
To His dawn. And one, the last of names,
Is quieter than these and keeps much less
Within it of the urgency of time
Caught crying in the pierce of it to her.
It is a simple place, and long sweet days
Are leisured in the usual and quiet
Heaven of its hours. O, here the slow
Growth came in long acceptancy and this
Place held for her a cherished dailyness.
The drone of summers and the sound of noons
Is in it, work, and doors, and treading feet,
The tables laid, the distances beyond
A window opened to the sun, and quick
Looks coming to her on an easy word
And laugh. The confidence, and all the good
Trust warm in spun robes hemmed for Him to wear.
It is a quiet name, and if she speaks
It now before the high place of the gathered
Wings where stars are set for crowns and all
The choiring of seraphim is clear,
It is a woman then who speaks and in
Her eyes the slow tides deepen and the word
Is uttered slowly in a woman's way

Who holds remembering. It is the place
Of Nazareth.

But only now a road
Is plain and winding on the hills slopes down
To where some white walls cluster in the sun
As she had known them, and had left them once
So long ago, and all the rich untaken
Gift of days is hidden yet and only
The white walls' look of calm as if no more
Had come to them or stirred about their roofs
Than wind and rain and what had always been,
Is promise now to her and sign of what
Lies waiting, and the Will that is content
With only waiting, and with only time.

And coming he dwelt in a city called Nazareth: that it might be fulfilled which was said by the prophets: That he shall be called a Nazarite.

Some old steps taken quickly and her hand
Is raised against a door that she had known.
A low word spoken, and the rush of words
That came of it in sudden cries across
A breathless space of pause, the tears, the laughter,
Names recalled that were more cries than names,
Her quick nod and the light of smiled assent,
The calls to others distantly, and arms
That took her, and her own arms that she gave
More eagerly for hunger and in loss
Of all restraint that these should be for her
To hold again. The eager words of Him
They spoke, rushed, tumbled words that came and came

Again when she had stood Him forward so,
And in a silence, let them look on Him.
O, there is no descended choice that ever
Chilled in her the common warmth or breathed
A mist to intervene between the earth
And where she walked. She wore no alabaster
Heart or held in it an innocence
That made it more than could be healed or struck
At in the common way, and if there had
Been loneliness, and still would be, as real
As any and as long, if far away
There would be courtyard and a hill, and streets
To stretch between in anguish sharp as stones,
Then kind days also might be granted her,
And she might live and strongly reach to them
With no more vague aloofness than is found
In lesser hearts and lesser innocence.
And this was home. These were the walls of home,
And these the voices that her thoughts had called
In exile sounding now for her to hear.
And she was glad for them. And for this moment
Was a woman. Welcomed. Only that.
Who hugged again within her little day
The strange, uncalculated joy of welcome,
And its pain.

She spoke of Egypt then,
And said without a too great eloquence
Or much profusion that it was a far
Place and the time was long she'd had of it.
Aye. After Bethlehem. They had been first
At Bethlehem. And there the Child had come.
The words then that she had been saying failed . . .

Until the quicker words that Joseph spoke
Had crossed her speech. They'd turned to him to hear
Of fears that rose at Bethlehem too soon
For his content in Herod, and of how
He'd taken her and fled beneath the night
And did not stop until he'd met a land
That was another land than Herod held.
The comprehending whispers answered him,
And now the dark tale of the swords still running
In the talk of cottages was told
Again more fearfully. But she could hear.
And Joseph too could hear. And what was said
Could fall across his muteness till he dared
To catch the drawn look white upon her face,
And note her hand that imperceptibly
Had sought unnoticed for the touch of Him.

They had returned. It was enough to say,
And whosoever heard could understand
It was enough, and was for them a fullest
Reason for the slow smile and the sigh
Of peace that could dismiss as past what fears
Had been or might have been, and wanderings
That were not looked for when they'd left these homes.
And they could turn and in the easy voice
That speaks a small familiar thing again,
More gently for the press of recent issues,
Ask of fields and woolens and the depth
Of wells, and what the signs were in the year
For grain, and what the promise was and price
For labor, and of needs they had; and find
The ease and confidence of small concerns

Was good to lean against and made the very
Weariness and yawns that grew of them
Seem comfort and assurance of return.

They rose then, and a last few kindly words
Were said of Him to her, and she could speak
Across her shoulder of her gratitude,
And give to Joseph's hand their gifts of oil
And eggs and linens and the wicks for lamps,
And take again beneath their lingered calls
An old path that was lonely for her tread.

She'd walked here once before, and knew this gate
That waited, and remembered it another
Day when there was singing and a few
Palms waved, and she had found his longer shadow
Cast ahead of her. It moved but slowly
Then and in the shade it made, she moved
Beside it trustingly, and knew his heart
For harbor and his arm for strong protection,
And the long brave humbleness that shaped
His virtue and had led him here, had caught
In that far day, a peace that came to her
Who only wondered whence would come the peace.
And peace was made again, and still was here
For her to take now that his shadow fell
Again across this path, and all the fears,
The lost uncertainties, and all the fretful
Plannings and the wait for pain, were gone
From her, and she had come with Joseph now
To bring Him where His house was on a path
In Nazareth.

A little door was closed
Behind her that was hers, and there was that
Within the thud and bolt of it that had
Not sounded in the other doors that closed
And were not hers, and she could find in it
A sound of ending, and a certainty
At last of long conclusion, and could rest
Against the stillness following as one
Returned where there were no more words for her
To hear and for a moment no demands.
And what was waiting in the dust to feel
Her touch was hers, and had not moved or changed,
And had not gained a different or altered
Aspect other than she knew, and still
Was here for her to come to, and to move
With deft expectancy that did not fumble
And was sure. And when the Child was laid
Not in His own place, but in some more hasty
Cot available beyond disturbance,
And a last sharp look and competent
Caress had made her certain of His ease,
She turned and was a woman made again
Secure, and in her quick unmeditated
Errands to the fires and scourings,
To drawers and cupboards and the place where kettles
Hung, to swift unfolding and refolding,
To the water jars and bins and racks,
She found a certainty that fell on her
At these familiar ways, and felt again
Within her mind that had not strayed too far
From watching Him, the warm good promises
Implicit in the tasks. Of quiet days,
And rest, and usualness, and nothing more

Than silence, and her heart to be the centre
For a trust of silence till the broken
Day when it should lift to take His wounds.

They did not take too long at what was left
For them to do, nor speak too much between
Themselves, nor note the stir and movement made
Beyond their threshold in the old unaltered
Sounds of Nazareth at dark, nor see
The lights of other homes dim down, as always
They had dimmed when they had had enough
Of waking for a while, but all of these
Unchanged were yet within the night and were
Not softened for a newer reverence,
Nor kept more meaning than they'd always made.
And only then another house was lost
To darkness in the night at Nazareth.

She heard Him breathing here. The little stirs
That came across His sleep, and must have thought
Then of the floors her hands had scrubbed so many
Times . . . of all the dishes laid behind
Their doors . . . and of her oven and the need
She had of hurrying with towels thrown
Across her arm, and where things were, and what
She'd always done with them . . . and how she had
No way to contemplate or guess what days
Might bring to Him. Here in the quiet night
She knew that she was home. And out of all
The timeless glory of His uncreated
Will, she held this pondering . . . Whose face
Unveiled would burn the staring eyes to pits . . .
He too was home. He too . . . Who was her Child!

And the child grew, and waxed strong, full of wisdom: and the grace of God was in him.

This is Luke again so briefly saying
Only what is given him to say.
A few words. Quiet. Almost casual
With such sweet reticence and sure observance
We may know who gave him them to say,
And let him span with unpretentious accent
And a simple speech, what all the young
Years held for her of dear remembering.
Her full gift of the days, the gracious wealth
That time spun golden in the long profusion
Of the afternoons, the years unhurried,
And the slow revolving spokes the seasons
Turned, the nights, the easy, uneventful
Dawns and unreluctant squanderings
Of moments, generous of after moments,
All her Nazareth is spoken here
So gently that it seems we hear a woman
Speak whose eyes are closed and who is saying
Slowly with a deep and secret smile
And with a nod . . . "Aye, then He grew. And gained
In strength . . . and . . ."

Luke of course has written down
What he had heard as once before in like
Simplicity he wrote of swaddling bands,
And only that she brought Him forth and laid
Him, crying, in a manger, and he has
Not written what he might have seen beneath
Her eyes that dreamed so deep of more than dreams.
There is so much of Him that is her own

To keep, and which must always be her own.
Forever. Held in the one heart that is hers,
And save in faint and unsubstantial shade
Of far analogy, unshared, unseen,
And uncommunicate beyond the single
Knowing laid so mute and unpartaken
In her love. This motherhood. This bond
And tie and blood that reached from her to Him.
What other eyes have watched Him so? What soul
Knew *this* of Him? What heart returned this look
Which only she might find? There might be words
She could relate to us, clear words with all
The meanings that we know yet held in them
And instant to our own increased reflection.
She might speak and we might hear, or Luke
Might plainly set them down for us to read,
And yet for all the words, the silences
Would be as deep and still would be not much
More said than what already has been said.
And so we only find this little phrase
To tell of all her years at Nazareth,
And what was waking in her eyes remains
Unuttered, silent, and inviolate.

The day when He had fallen and had turned
With bruises on His wrists and she had seen
The teared dismay that went so easily
When she had taken Him and washed the pain.

The first sound of His voice in praise of God!

She must have marked that moment? When His lips
First faintly spoke in prayer and she had heard
The glory that had sounded on His breath?

Or some warm dusk when He had laughed above
The others and had shouted in the chant
Of children's games.

And then, she may have kept
An odd detached scene bright within the flow
Of all the years, some little moment only
When she sat with mending on her lap,
And held a small, worn garment up to find
That it was torn. And suddenly her eyes
Filled, and her hand was trembling when she thought
Whose seam she sewed and Whose the broken thread!

The birthdays that she marked and looked for stars
That only rose again within His eyes.

And when the feasts came and she spoke of them.
And when He went with Joseph and looked up
At Israel and she observed Him standing
In the sombre shawls and listening. . . .

These are the times, these feasts of Israel
That are so marked for her, when all the old
Ways of her race took sharper and more poignant
Meaning as they moved about His head.
They'd stirred the sons of Abraham so long
A time, these feast days rising, that they came
Now from the past like winds above a field
Of grain to bend them in obedience
To old expected urging that could move
Them in a single impulse unresolved
And unprotesting. She had watched for them,
And kept the mellowed rituals with more

Than distant faithfulness, and did not find
The chanted mercies nor the grave enacted
Signs of testament so cold or formal
That her heart might not catch up more warmly
What was told in them that she could know
Need be no longer told. And one of these
Is set across her years like sudden speech
Resuming quietly when we had heard
So long but silence, and no uttered sound.

And when he was twelve years old, they going up into Jerusalem according to the custom of the feast, and having fulfilled the days, when they returned, the child Jesus remained in Jerusalem; and his parents knew it not.

Some concentrate and strain of interest,
A mood, a need, some dominating wish
Can hold a city fixed, and for a while,
Locked in to sudden order, till the core
Of wholeness breaks and scatters it again
Beyond its unison to loud relaxing.
Then released confusions and the shouts
And movements of uncentred multitudes
Are loosed along the streets to lift conflicting
And recrossing wills, and throngs that had
Been drawn of many roads and settled down
For brief preoccupation, rise to seek
The roads again. And in Jerusalem
A nation, thickened for some days and dense
About the Temple, turned and thinned itself
In moving streams that would outflow along
The farthest roads until the distant towns
And provinces could feel their final ebb,

And pool the slow diminished last of them.
We must not think these feast times were a neat
And tidy movement down a marbled aisle.
This was no meagre pageant, nor a thin
Procession with a few to walk in it.
This was the gathering of tribes, the call
And rising of a race. Josephus speaks
Of millions, and they moved and prayed and moved
Again like millions. Strong. And lusty. Real
With needs of people treading on a road,
With carts and tents and stores and all the packs
Of journeying; and when the caravans
For Galilee were gathered up and straggled
Out again, returning down through Beeroth,
She was walking, and was one unmarked
And lonely in a throng, and only glad
There had been covenant, and soon would be
The first halt made when she might come again
To Joseph and to Him. There was some singing,
Sounds that swelled and faded on the march,
Some talk, some sighs of weariness, and all
About, the good feel of security
In neighbors found and caught again along
The road and in regathered company.
There may have been in her a slightest stir
And sense that she was walking here alone,
Some brief distraction in the speech she gave
To friends, and in the songs, and some quick glances
Made half searching at the rush of children's
Steps. But this was always so, and now
It was no greater ache or lack, or feel
Of incompletion than she'd always known
When He was absent and her eyes might not

Be filled of Him and what she heard be only
What He said. She'd learned of this too long
Ago to mark it now within her heart
As strange that when He'd gone to other places,
There was not much left for her to wedge
Between the waiting and remembering.

She walked here in the dust among the rest
Of Galilee, and looked far on ahead
To where the lines were circling and the carts
And beasts and gear were breaking from the ranks,
And families were joined to set their tents
Against the night and stake their own plots out
And light their fires. She hurried then and raised
Her eyes more eagerly to search for Joseph's
Form, and turned within her mind what food
She knew was wrapped among his packs and could
Be had for them. And in a little while,
She found him waiting with his hand upon
The beast and smiling as he watched for her.

She'd grown to know this air and attitude
That graced him here, when unobserved she saw
Him standing by the road. It was the sharp,
Unconscious profile of his eagerness,
And all the gift of him that she'd received
So many times. She'd learned this light that rested
On his face, and seen before the lift
His head made when he watched for her. And now
She did not need more than the instant's glance
To find it clear, and find again what strain
Was on him stronger than was usual.
It was not much. Only that she'd caught

A look of too great searching, and a trace
In him of too intense expectancy.
As if a faint fear waited to be laid.
No more than tiredness, except she knew
That it was more, and when she ran a little
Step or so, and turned from where the women
Walked to let him see, she marked his quick
Enkindled gladness break to sudden light
And then withhold itself. And in her heart
Before his voice asked or his eyes were sure,
She felt the first chill closing of the cold.

Her silent searching came to him and found
But other searching here that was his own.
It was as if she'd stepped from out some shading
And had found a warm expected light
Had failed and she was yet in shadow. Only
That a sound had not been heard, and now
No laughter came when she had waited laughter.
Not too much of pain or sudden fall
Of emphasis upon the threat of it.
No cries. No anguish. Only little words
Half uttered, and inquiring, and the fears
That started unadmitted in their eyes.
And reassuring smiles and tones that held
The ominous afar in obvious
Dismissals caught at and brought up too quickly
For complete achievement. Only that,
And the swift unspoken and too certain sense
That these few rugs and hampers might be left
Here by the road and they might go without
More thorough settlement to seek for Him,
And call the word back formed already on

Their lips that one had found Him, when the smiles
Might leap between more honestly and deep
Good laughter be relief that was unsaid.

She turned and found her swift steps hesitant
For certainty. It pounded in her mind
And paused her breathless while the beat of it
Broke down the world and left her pitched and blinded
In a darkness where there was no world.
It had not fallen till she turned from Joseph
Then. But this was searching now . . . a search . . .
He had been lost! She'd lost Him! She had lost . . .
Until the world returned, and wavering
She fixed upon the old persuasive moving
Of familiar forms to drag denials
To her heart and stand them firmer there.
These were her friends. Her people. These were faces
She had always seen, and this the calm
Road she had walked so many times. And all
The way it had been so. And children followed
On in no more strange companionship
Than what they met behind their own closed gates.
And found in all their homes. She looked again,
And in a friend's quick casual nod, discerned
A deprecating and assuring sameness
Warm enough to raise in her a brave
And half amused dismissal of the fears,
That would have seemed conviction had it asked
Of her a less determined hold on it,
Or had endured unfaltered past the first
Few aimless steps. He did not run to her.
Or suddenly call out her name beyond
The next more likely tents, and none had come

Who saw her pass to speak of Him without
The asking. She had marked that. There were none
Who spoke of Him. And when she'd asked and asked
Again, and found concern that had been kind,
But gave no firmer answer than another's
Unconcern, and moved away and moved
Away, she did not hear her faint voice speaking
Fainter, fainter words that were the same
Words that were only words, and held no longer
Brightness or the strength of unrebuffed
Expectancy, and fell against the growing
Hollows of the dark in smaller sound,
And smaller sound that dwindled till the dark
Had gulfed them and had left her there with all
Her asking ended. Stilled. With no more steps,
And no more words, and eyes that only saw
The dark and that no seeking movement came,
Nor answer, nor responding, nor reply.

The others' voices and the closed, contented
Camps she trailed past for the slowed return,
The good relaxing of them, and the snug
Security of faces near a fire
Were unintended pain. They cast rebukes
At her she took more sharply for their silent
Guiltlessness. These circles here. These limits,
Sure and guarded. They were condemnations.
Condemnations. She could sense the line
And boundary of them. These folded folk.
These gathered, counted ones who were not lost.
She walked here, shut away. Who had no Child!
Who had no Child! And did not know this moment . . . !

Then no longer slow directed steps,
But sudden running feet that stumbled, stumbled,
Running with the wild cries choked within
Her throat, and tears that stung, and wilder needs
That sought for Joseph, Joseph now, for Joseph . . .

He was there for her to find again,
Waiting while his heart watched in his eyes,
And did not need more than his first quick sight
Of broken poise, the tangled shawls, and brow
That creased above the twisting pain, to know
He saw in one burned instant more than all
He'd prayed against, and more than what he thought
The stars or he would ever come to look on
While the earth held and his eyes were whole.
She staggered once, and he was near to hold
Her then, and take her sobs in stripes across
His mind that would be cut there till his grave,
And after it. This was not sound that sods
Could stuff. This was her crying who had never
Cried. This was a new pain, quivered, broken
To the air from innocence that felt
The blades that barb the damned. This cry was loss.
Not pain, but loss. And in it, there was more
Than all her Calvary he would not see.
She shook with it, and shivered in the shock
That broke her strength and bent against his arms
Still trembling, and the winds that moved on her
And touched her tears and took these deep, too muted
Sobs, might bring them in the night across
The hills to stir the little leaves that waited
In His garden place of olive trees!

He did not speak, and did not try, and knew
Too surely what the comfort was he had
Such need to bring and could not bring, and that
His heart and words that came of it were pithed
And emptied of their ease and were but shells
And stalks and bitter rinds until he spoke
The one word that was not now his to say.
Yet he was here. And by that much was wanted,
And could clutch a smaller gratitude
That it was so, and in the moments then
That turned in him when there was only lostness,
And the long moans drawing on her deep,
Spent breath, the pain that he had always known
Had ached beneath his love and was an essence
Untransmuted and inseparate
From it, attained a dry and utter anguish,
Bitterer than could be laid in tears,
And centred was the pain he might not hold
All pain, and grief he might not take her grief
And keep it only his. But he could not,
And thought again of old and lesser moments
When he'd learned that he could not, and that
He might have said a word, or turned his head,
Or used a wiser prudence to have held
This grief away from her had he the strong
Intensity he'd promised once to keep.

He'd caught that in her sobs, and knew that pain
Alone could not have honed and edged them so,
And told himself, and with a broken gesture,
Tried to tell to her, it should be his,
Not hers, it should be his, that in her heart
Regret was scalding and the cries and taunts

Of accusation rose. It was not hers
To watch, and they had found no threat or reason
Or a change in custom, or a fear
That would have been neglect had they not seen.
He'd found more words now. And the rush of them
Was eager till they fell again and came
To silence weighted in the uselessness
Of words they'd never used and never searched
To use, and did not find now too convincing.

He was lost. The dull sound turned again
And was repeated. He was lost. Lost.
Her sobs were stopped, and darkened lines were deep
Upon her face, and in her eyes, an older
Sadness when she slowly lifted them,
And some small stooping in her fragile form
That would be now forever there. She knew
What road was hers and when the lonely tread
Of it began, and in the smothered ache,
She did not ask why he was folding robes
And tying girths, but only watched him there,
And gave into his hand a strap he'd dropped,
And followed after when he'd turned into
The night. And saw the stars were not the stars
Of Bethlehem.

Nor was the road the road
To Bethlehem, nor any road that she
Had walked on, and the crunch of tired steps,
The slow, aloof sound of the ass's hoofs,
And all the silences that lay between
With no sound in them and no words, was more
Of lostness. This was ache that had no feel

Or sight of Him to make it seem much less
Than pain. This was a road that could not be.
A place that was not. This was darkness come
When she was waked and pushed beyond the edge
Of possibles, and clutched with scratching fingers
At the stones of dreams. This was a screech
Shrieked down in fever from the topmost swirls
Of night. He was not here! *He was not here!*
Alone! Not here! She'd lost Him. She had lost . . .
But these were steps that she was stumbling out
And making in a noise that she could hear
Beyond denial. She could turn and find
The quilted caravans behind had grown
So dim that they had merged with vaguer fogs,
And she had walked here far from them. And was
A woman only who had borne a Child,
And now was here and did not have the Child.

It struck her then that others too were moving.
She'd not thought of this, but there were others
In the night. There might be more who preyed
On stragglers and were less concerned with law
And how a Child might cry than with a price
He'd bring, and how a stroke might break His lips
Of mild protesting. She had heard it so,
And in the fear, she heard again His voice.
How it might speak and what the sound might be
Of pleading, and the need for her! And stopped
To strain the dark and with her pulses running,
Pulled the distance in to search for cries.
And then moved on, moved on again more slowly
With the cold assurance that there were

No sounds and only roads that had no clearer
Meaning than the fears.

They'd come upon
A few odd wanderers like thicker dark
That loomed up suddenly more near to them.
And they had paused a moment while the horses
Neighed, and voices spoke to them in answer
Strangely for the question they had asked.
No, they'd not seen a Child, nor found a Child
Who'd looked to them. And when they'd gone beyond,
And speech and murmured echo then had passed
Into the night, her lifted search was ended,
And the hopes that only were half hopes,
And scanned their faces wearily, died down
Again, and were no more than further pain
That stirred a little to become more keen.

No need of fear, or if the mind could hold
For long remembrance of the speech of angels
Uttered when the swords of Herod shook,
There could be found some cause to cancel fear;
Enough, at least, to threaten it in careful
Reasons urged and set against the heart.
He was not lost while all the legions watched
Who sang for Him. It still was true He kept
Within Him secrets broken from the molds
Of stars. He still had come of prophecy
And knew the spaceless lanes before the world.
But there had been so long no stars, nor songs,
Nor glories trailing, other than the musing
Of a Child. He had been playing now

So long a time. And she had watched Him grow,
Had sewed for Him, had come to recognize
His taste in food, had seen Him flushed and thirsty,
And had heard of Him such simple words
Of sun and rain and how the blades cut freshly
In the fragrant boards. And for so long
A time she'd seen the unstrung sandals resting
In her home! And this was shattering
Of reasons and denial that the claws
Of fear be any less than what was torn
In her. This was a rout for all persuasions.
And the length of days when He'd not looked
To angels but to her, and had not cried,
Nor asked except that she might hear, became
New goads to dig a deeper pain and hurry
Her and sting her mind against the lags
Of hope and would not let her sink among
Assumed conclusions for a space of peace,
Nor give again to angels what had been
Her own.

The Child was hers, and over her
She heard again her own voice that had said
He should be hers, and should be met and held
And guarded in what life was hers to give
Until there was no more in her of life
Or gift He did not have. She'd said that once.
The sound of it was still upon her ears.
"O, be it done to me." It followed her
And moved before her, and the winds were filled
Of it. "O, be it done to me." The pledge
Of care. The promise and the gift of all
The shreds and strengths that were her own to give!

The word of fealty and care before
A trust. She'd said that. She had said that once.
And now she walked here, emptied of the trust,
And lost. And somewhere, lonely, He was crying . . .
And she was not near to minister!

The dark road twisting had no step in it
That was not old for her in liftless pain.
Beyond all tears and set beyond increase
Or any rise or fall, as if her heart
Had always known the beat of this that moved
In her and chilled her like a colder blood
That now was hers and always had been so.
No single step that was not now but one
More taken in so many that the road
Might be a thousand, and be yet the same
Road with the same pain made not more or greater
Than was stilled and held and weighed and steadied
Till the night was leaden with the mass
Of it, and burdened downward in the dark
Beneath the dull reliefless press where only
Prayers were life and memories were hopes,
She moved beyond the last plain and the last
Hill, and had seen ahead the towered walls
Of wide Jerusalem.

The emptiness
And quiet here so strangely left along
The streets that had been spilling with the throngs,
The air and feel of dark, the few dim, lonely
Lights that burned, the scattered litter blown
Against the stones and trampled in the path
Of many feet, the silences, the freedoms

At the corners where the day had raised
Such haste, the distant, nameless sounds, and then
The lost sound of their own small movement, made
A muted wandering for her that held
Too much of edge to be a dream, and yet
The vagueness was of dreams. She knew this place.
She'd passed here when the sun was warm. She'd gone
Away. She'd turned her back on this and found
The road that was departure, and had joined
The songs of confidence and heard the talk
Of home that had forgotten that these streets
Were visible, or that they were. But now
It was not so, and time and roads and steps
Were turned and twisted to an eerie strangeness,
And there was no home, nor any road
To home, and she was walking in the streets,
And where she should not be, and wandering
In hollows where the doors were closed, and only
Winds were moving in the lonely dust.
They could not tell for certainty what new
Direction might be best or where the way
Was that might lead to one less aimless sign
Than might be brought by any other path.
And standing in the chill, and whispering,
They only found within their strained and tired
Voices, words that were the forced conjectures
Of their needs and piecing out of hopes,
So wearied in the withering of fears
They were not hopes so much as wish for them.

He caught the hard aloofness of the walls
That fronted them, the bland and uncommitted
Staring of the doors, the slats of windows,

Unresponsive and impersonal
As stones, and looking on them, sensed a maze
Of places unrevealed in crisscross streets.
He did not have a ready answer rising
To his lips or strong decisions made
To give to her in plans and ordered searchings
That were sure. He had no buoyant heart
For meeting questions, nor the strength to bolster
Confidence, but in the dark he felt
Her eyes that turned to him and knew the hope
That waited plans, and out of that was strong.
He took a firm step with a word of search
That might be now no longer than a place
That sheltered them some little while ago.

They came to it, and Joseph was not bold
In knocking nor in words that asked but one
Replying now. He stood expectant here,
While sudden, shrill, protesting voices, pitched
To sharp annoyance found and answered him.
They'd seen no Child. There had been some, a dozen
More or less, but they'd been gone a whole
Half day's length. No, no, none had since returned.

It fell on her and for a moment left
Her moveless and it seemed she had not heard,
Or only followed with a slowed attention
What her heart had known before the first
Denial fell. He was not here. She knew
That, and the word of it was only more
Of pain that dropped unnoticed to a brimmed
Receiving whole and mingled till the anguish
Was as one and spilled across a cup

Too deep and bitter for her lips, except
The plea that met it was so old it came
To her from out the old prayers of her days,
And was so new it made a new acceptance
And a dark partaking prophecy:
If it be possible, let this now pass,
But not my will, but Thine, but Thine be done!

She turned away. There was no more to seek.
And in the faint hope's curled and withering
Defeat was emptiness, and loss too great
For what the hope had been, save that it moved
So long before her, it had seemed much more
Than what she knew it was, and feigned a strength
In that it was alone. There were no others
Now. No alternates or further choice.
There was nothing now. He was not here.
They had not found His place, nor knew if any
Place might now be found that would be His.
The world was here and all the deadened dark
That lay on it, but worlds were wastes and spread
Away too vast and pointless for the mind's
Perception, and the dark was only dark.
She moved a little, and her hand reached down
To find her packs once more, until she heard
The voice of Joseph speaking and the words
He said were of a rest, and sleep, he seemed
To urge for her. She heard him. It was rest
He said, and something of the dawn and light
That would be coming after it, and that
There was no further place, and only need
Of wait and prayers and resting for a while.

She marked a kindness that surrounded her,
And how suspicious voices, thick with sleep,
Had risen suddenly to other word
Of welcome in an understanding not
Too far removed from what was true, and he
Was speaking for her of a gratitude.

And she was glad for him. It had been long
Since he had rested, and his strength was worn.
And oddly then her heart turned to this warmth
And care that came to them when He was gone.
They'd searched within another night and had
Not found such care. But only broken stalls
Within a stable. And they'd fled once. Fled
Away. And He was there to cry. But now
He was not here. Not here. And they were welcomed,
When the last need that she had was welcome.

She was grateful, and a few brief, tired
Words hid all but that, and briefer wants
Were granted, and the silence came again
About the cold place where her heart was held.
Joseph knew that it was good for her
To rest. And sleep perhaps. And pray without
The roads to stare at her; and felt among
His own pleas and the deep upsurging wave
Of all his prayers what he had heard, so low
And muffled that it almost was not clear.
It was a sob. Not long, nor broken deep
Across the pain. So faint and quiet now,
His breath was caught before his mind was sure.
But it *was* sobbing. Hers.

And then he knew
What cried here in the ancient sound of all
The loneliness of earth. This was a sleep
That came on her beyond the closing fall
Of other nights. Aye. This was new. Defeat.
He was not here. Her head was laid, the first
Time where He was not near to her!

The day
That followed hides from us within a phrase
That lets us see in Luke's quick reticence
No more than that it was, and that it held
A place among her sum of days, as if
She sighed it in remembrance, and Luke heard
And marked it down in such brief words it is
Quite possible to pass it quickly by,
As once her breath dismissed it, and to lose
The pain and length of it in what has not
Been said. But it was there, this day, and was
Not swiftly lived or brought to end. Light
Was on it, light that rose above the scabbard
Of the dark horizon like a sword
To slit again in new relentlessness
Old scars that sleep had almost turned to dreams.
It was a harder light, so long and steadied
In the harsh glare held above her head.
She stared at it and found no moment's rescue
Or relief. Red rimmed, her eyes had turned
The pain back blinding in the search that met
This day and moved across the squares and down
The crowds, turned past the corners, and the walls
Of stone, and strained along the streets for sight
Of Him, and when the long hours, drawn and brassed

In unresponse, had grown to hammered shafts
That pressed on her and gave no edge but anguish,
And no sign that might be grasped and bent
Unto another hope, her feet dragged slower
In the dust and slower, slower, paused,
And for a little she was then a woman,
Broken, and her lost heart cried within
Her in the dry sob that could find no voice
Or tears, or further strength for search, or any
Ease.

The high pitched, strident sounds of markets
Rose around her, unconcerned, and tides
Of murmurous and shrill inconsequence,
And words and scraps of speech, and shouts, detached
And meaningless, were swirled like waves about
Her lonely silence, and the wash and cease,
And wash of them made more of loneliness
For her who was not spoken too, nor seen,
Nor heeded much, and only stood so small
And indeterminate. So lost. So stilled.

She'd searched so many faces now, had stared
At children, had beseeched so many names
And doors, had followed in the trace of guessed
And plausible conjectures, prayed and watched,
And prayed again, had asked so many times,
Had turned and searched again and found the same
Refusal in the same streets that had first
Refused. . . .

Her closed eyes opened, and the steps
That wearied in the dust could not resume,

Moved on again, and Joseph walked with her,
And did not choose or challenge with a question
What the street was that they turned, but walked,
And only found that twilight came again
And that her step was slow.

Another night
Descended and the stain of dark was spreading
Like a sombre wound that bled slow shadows
Deepening. They were not hopeful then,
And in a learned submissiveness, they watched
The shadows mingled widening, and knew
This was an end of day and was for them
An end of what the day had hoped, and now
There would be only dark, and now no more
Of hope but only waiting in the night.
This was not fear. The loss had grown too numbed
For that, and was a deader thing than pain.
Too much of search and certainty and dull
Rebuttal and too long, too long, a bearing
Of the loss had gone before this dark
To let it seem another fall than deadness.
She was weighed with it, and held it heavy
And unsobbed and unrelieved and tired
On her heart, and all her pitiful
And ceaseless seeking, and the emptied gain
Of it, and all rebuffs, and all the flames
Of smothered hopes that rose and died so quickly
And so many times, were heaped and massed
Upon the hard remaining lack of Him,
That was a darkness deeper than the dark,
And in this night was colder than the cold
That shrouds the dead.

And if there were a part
Within her that was living still, that stirred
And moved and lifted to the weight of pain,
It was her prayers and that strong innocence
Of will that had refused that she should die.

And it came to pass, that after three days they found him in the temple sitting in the midst of the doctors, hearing them and asking them questions.

There could have been no promise in the dawn,
No lifting of her loss or sudden sense
That this was all that would be asked of her.
For all she dared to hope, the yesterday
Might be a life, and this but one more added
In a long forever. One had passed,
And there was nothing here to say that this
Was other than she'd found and would not be
The prelude to one more, and that to more,
Until there were no days or nights, or sleep
Or waking, only more and more and more,
And ache and emptiness. There was no sign
Of surcease here, but only light to strain
Again in search.

How far the day was drawn,
Or what the winnowing of space, or long
Repeated carefulness, we do not know.
They moved near to the Temple. They had been
There many times, as they had been to many
Places many times, but there was that
That turned them to the courts and porticoes,
And restlessly could not be satisfied

Or ended. It was more than reasoning,
And more than fitness, and her thoughts returned
Insistently, and of a will they had
Beyond her, when her feet were wandering,
And in the search she'd gone to farther streets.
An air was here. A sense. An instinct hid
Within her heart that made her lift and hark
For sound of Him.

Such movement and such flow
Of colored robe. So much of ritual
And teaching. Down the corridors, the steps,
Within the porches where she'd seen the groups
Debating words and where the masters were
Who spoke of Israel. Her search had touched
Their fringes, and had skirted them before.
There was a larger group who held a hushed
Intentness. More of masters clustered here.
And one among them had been questioning.

And then she heard a Voice that answered him!

And that was all. One spoken sound that fell
Across her tired heart and settled there.
Her eyes closed and the tense, arrested strain
Of listening was slowly eased and tears
Had come. She swayed a little and her lifted
Hand unfolded, falling, and her breath
Was stilled. It is. *It is*. The world was that.
And life and tiredness and skies and lights,
And shadows, sounds, and all the silences.
There was no more than that. It is. *It is*.
No earth, nor walls, nor brimming tears, nor dust,

Nor pain, nor anything. But only this.
It is. And in the bright annihilate
That tore the past down and the world, and left
No consequence or further flow beyond
Itself to be a future or another
World, there was but one simplicity
So clear and lucid and enveloping
It made in time a centred, moveless earth
Where she was standing, and His voice was all
Of her.

She could not go at once to claim
Him for her hunger and to ease the long
Defeated ache in grasp and hold of Him.
There was no generosity or ease
In freedom that could let her rush to Him
And sob above His hair. He was not hers
To take in good forgetfulness and hold
In gathered infancy. These were the masters
Here, and she was distant at the edge
Of them, and small, not daring more than nearness,
And the little moves that let her see
Between them, peering, in a hungry look
That waited for another sound of Him.
She did not cry. And how much more of words
There was for her to hear and eagerly
To catch as drops upon her parched mind, thirsty
For a further speech, and how much more
Of waiting, is not written down for us
To read. But it was long enough for her
To note and to remember He was sitting
In the midst of them, and that He asked
Them questions, and they wondered at Him so.

And they had marked a wisdom that had set
Them whispering, and that they harked to Him.

Did some brief sign of His reveal her then,
And notice her so that they stood aside
And let her pass, and murmured she was one
Who came for Him? Was there a bond and yearning
In her love so strong that they could sense
Her presence and were quiet at the tears
And haggard griefs? Or was it just the end
Of words and that they turned and did not see,
As they were passing, two who did not turn?
Luke has not said, and only we have known
That after all the roads and all the sobs,
And after all eternities of time
And pains and prayers, and after shattering
Of worlds, the worlds were made again, and she
Was freed to Him.

Son, why hast thou done so to us? behold thy father and I have sought thee sorrowing.

This is the dark sob uttered in the psalms
That she is speaking out. And He will shake
It from His lips and tear the nailed night jagged
With the same prayer pleading to the pain
Above His cross, and He will speak the same
Abandonment. And none will be to answer
Him save as His heart hears of itself,
And as she, standing near to Him, may know
Who will remember then her broken plea,
And find it echoed in His own.

But now,
It is no more than what a woman says
Who hugs a Child, and loses in the pain
And joy of that, all else but this return
Of motherhood, and if a mystery
Is made, it is an old and common one.
And if again reflecting, we can find
A boldness and some shading of complaint
That comes to touch her words, we must not lose
The depths of ease, the unstrained confidence
From which she cried, and hear again the sound
As it was deepened in the sobs and choked
From her with all her claims and needs and fears
That were her right to speak. This is a word
That many sons have heard, and have not found
Too hard to understand. And He was hers,
And she was only saying He had gone,
And spoke from out the days of Nazareth,
And from the pain that may be measured now
Since she would name it, who would not cry out
At Egypt, and who shall be silent, silent
Ever more.

And then the first words fall
That we have heard of Him. He knew her heart,
And in a long past He had entered there
And lingered in the one clear sanctuary
Given Him of earth beyond rebellion.
O, He knew the gifts that flawlessly
Were His, of praise and love so strongly worn
That He might look upon her face and need
Not turn away, and need not grant to her

Of any mercy. And He knew her pain
That was not alien to Him, nor left
Aside these days when He had gone from her.
We hardly think of that. But He had come
To wear our garments and to touch our blood,
And therefore could be lonely in the need
Of her. And so He answered to the cry.

How is it that you sought me? did you not know that I must be about my father's business?

The sudden quiet came. Deep. So deep
That time and breath and joy and thought were lost.
No more. No added words. No more. No more.
A closed finality that found in her
A woman wrapped in silence and the wait
Of silence was her heart that heard, that heard
His speaking, but had mostly heard the thunder
Of the quiet, and the after pause
When there was nothing more that He would say.

How is it that you sought me? did you not know that I must be about my father's business?

The echoes turned in her, the fading echoes
Of His words and of the sound of them
So deep in uttered tenderness. It held
Against remembering, and was not flawed,
Nor marred by any tone of altered love,
Nor did it show an edge that could be made
Into denial or a hard disdain
Of her. She heard the sound in what He said,

And knew it was the same He'd grown to use
In any speech intended for her heart.
But she had heard the meanings on His words
Beyond His tone. And they were there unchanged,
And turning in an echo that could not
Be muted now. "Did you not know? Not know?"
It bent her eagerness so sternly back
To what she'd fled from, and was holding her
To stare in unremitting clarity
At what was meant. No mist and no deceiving
Drifted in to cloud His words to vaguer
Senses. They were plain. So starkly plain.
This distance. This aloneness and the hurt
Of space, the yearning that had drained the days
She'd thought were ended and were filled again.
This was a prospect, this was future here,
And it was not to pass. It would be hers,
This bleakness, and she'd lived a concentrate
And bitter essence in this severing
That one day would be cut again and drawn
Across her dreams and wakings for a longer
Pain. This was her way, and she could see
The broken shards that waited for her feet.

His Father's business. Aye. For always that.
But now without her. She must understand.
Without her. It was something that her hands
Might not reach out to find with Him and mold
In good obedience. He'd be alone.
The words said that and she had heard them now.
This vigiled ache, this loneliness and night
Bereft of stars when she had cried so darkly:
This was what it was to be!

They stood
So quietly and with such air of held
Suspended things, there might have been a flow
Of silence longer than the throbs of time
Can measure or endure; till Joseph spoke
Of haste and roads that still were waiting them
To Nazareth. The hush was gentle then,
And simple words were uttered easily,
And lighting smiles had come to almost hide
The inner shadows moving in their eyes,
But naught of shyness nor the strained defeat
Of ease, nor any cold constraint that cast
A reticence about their older ways.
They were not more aware of Him. No new
Attainment of a reverence had reached
Them that had not been clear, and only now
More certain portents shone within the day,
And she had found another kind of tears.
His words were dreams, and stars, and shepherds' feet
Again, and swords, and Simeon's avowal
Brought more near, and in a sudden speech
Made imminent. They had not thought that none
Would fall again. But greater gift was asked
In what she'd heard, and deeper draught of pain.
And she'd been waiting. For the long years now
She had been waiting. Only loneliness
Was new.

Quite simply they were speaking on
Of passage and the need for hurrying,
Of robes and of His sandals to be tied
Securely, and she noticed then how tall
He stood to Joseph's height.

She came to Him
And kissed Him. He had turned to her to take
Some bundle from her burden for His own.

There could have been no more than that, nor more
Of evidence or prophecy to halt
Their steps and falter them in stern design.
And what is written speaks but of return,
That now He was a Child Who walked with them.
They'd found the steps, and turned into the lanes,
And they were three who were of Nazareth,
And were departing now to reach a home.

The echoes turned in her, the fading echoes
Of His words, and of the end of them
That kept such mystery. When would He go?
And where? Would she have sight of Him again?
Would ever in the darkness come a day
When He might stop to give a moment's surcease
To the pain? And would she die of pain
And fail Him? Had she failed Him? Had she failed . . .
Was this the reason she would be forever
Far from Him? Her meagre heart rejected
Since it was not great enough? What roof
Would keep Him when He'd gone from her? What skies?
His Father's business. Would she know of that?

And they understood not the word, that he spoke unto them. . . . And his mother kept all these words in her heart.

Joseph was remembering the fall
Of quiet accent on the word He'd said

About His Father, and he'd marked the sure
Inclusion of himself and of his heart
When she'd said first they had been searching Him.
It was the only bliss he'd ever hoped,
This name, and strength, and head he was for them.
And when at Nazareth they'd come to him
And gave precedence and had asked decisions
For his home, when she'd deferred to him,
And He had raised His eyes and asked consent,
Joseph was not dull nor uninformed
Of what his honor was. This was a name
That gave his arms good strength and warmed his mind
To prayer. It was his life to be for Him
A father. Joseph swore then he would break
Two hands in labor, wear them to the stumps
Of hands if He would ask or ever breathe
One whispered wish. But He had gone from him,
And said it was His Father's business here
That took Him, and He'd be alone. The words
Said that, and he had heard them all. His Father's . . .

Joseph spoke again and said they might
Attain so far as Beeroth while the day
Was holding if they were not wearied now.

The words that moved again across his mind,
The sight of masters standing, and the air
They had of reverence, these are the sum
For him of miracles. This was to be
The end of all he'd see of signs and wonders
And the growth of Him; he is to have
No seat at Cana's table, and the place
Of resurrection shall not find him glad.

This is the end. His fingers will not close
Upon the thorns, nor will the wounds be scarred
Upon his eyes. This is the end, and after
This we shall not find him on the page
That tells of her. Joseph walks a road
And brings them home; he will be waiting there
A while, and for a little he will speak
Directions and be heard, and he will guide
Young hands in building scaffolds and the beams
And doors much smaller than He'd builded once
Of space. But he will see no more than this.
And walking now, his gospel has been heard.

She was grateful that they'd go beyond
The city's edge and hoped the winds across
The hills would be fresh sweet with fragrances
And cool. She wanted strong things, and the sight
Of skies again, that she might see them bend
Above His hair.

XII

THE heart that holds great gifts within itself
Keeps silence, and it does not whisper on
Of secret satisfactions, nor peruse
Its triumphs in a hid complacency.
The deepness is too filled and much too wide
For that; and if she'd learned to gather in
The least light on His face, and hoarded merest
Shadows of His form, and hugged the sight
Of Him returned and given her again . . .
And if the pain had been accepted now
And pressed into her joys as equal joy,
Still nothing more than this had come to her,
And in her heart no other consciousness.
She did not turn reflecting to the tribute
That He could be walking so and moved
Now down a road with her, that she had gained
Here newer dignity, that this return
Was eminence and brighter glory set
Within a cap of stars. She did not think
Of dignity, or crowns, or deep implied
Submissions, or of honors laid in them,
But only knew that she was eased with Him
Again, that she was whole, and certain, calmed
In Him, and did not look beyond to what
Is given her and what is said of her
That He would put away omnipotence
And walk beside so quietly, and listen
To command.

But it is there, and we
May not be unobservant and must see
It plainly. It is clear. And one look or
A thousand will reveal the same thing Luke
Is saying quietly about the end
Of this swift episode of breaking clouds.
Israel had heard a new Voice speak
Before its Temple. Wisdom brimmed and trembled
Out a few drops falling from the fuller
Floods. And men were eager, thirsting, thirsting
For the draught of Him. And she had heard
About His Father's business, had been asked
Why she had searched. He'd not been lost. Not lost.
This was a moment which the prophecies
Had waited and the years had hoped, but now
One consequence had come, no more than this,
He turned, a Child again, her Child, and walked
With her to where her small roof was, and home.

And he went down with them, and came to Nazareth: and was subject to them.

It is a summary a man might make
Within a phrase, who had been hearing only
Of simplicities, the one brief word
That could be written after he had harked
In wonder to the long sweet counting over
Of her days, and to the unaffected
Telling that they ran so gently on
That no sign came of them, nor dominance
Beyond the manner of all homes where young
Sons are who wait for stature and give strong
Obedience. This is a word that might

Be said of any hearth, and since it is
Not said of any hearth but of His own,
Tells more of her than all the praises strung
Together endlessly, and more than stiff
Superlatives our poor minds might conceive
For speech of her. It is as if Luke's hand
Had lifted, and he dreamed upon the quiet
Accents of her voice, that he was lost
In more than what was said in her account,
And he could see beyond her words and find
The vision of a grandeur that she told
So simply now, and so unconsciously.
She had been wreathed in deference He gave,
Had worn the garlands of His good response,
Had been the rule, the mistress of His way,
She'd spoken to Him, and had heard reply
That gave such tribute and such haloing.
And now Luke saw he had no rhetoric,
Nor any mounting words to tell of this,
And sighing, wrote the one phrase that could hold
It plain: that He was subject unto them.

O, here is Nazareth, and all the long
Years of His love. This is the deeper praise
He gave Who shall not choose a lesser word,
Nor utter easy honors when they will
Come near to ask Him in a future time.
This is His soundless hymn, and He has made
It hers. He hath thus magnified her soul.

A woman wrapped in silence. Deep. So deep,
The far heart dares not listen, dares not hear.
This is her own. This silence is her own.

The feet of God move softly to her call.
He speaks no praise. He is obedient.

Had there been centuries, she would have caught
At time to hold the least swift flow of it
As fingers close upon quick waters running
In the sun. Had there been years unmeasured,
Prodigal, and filled with futures made
Unlimited, she would have found no moment
Laggard or unshod with flight, but it
Was not so, and these days were preyed upon,
And caught by dusk too hungrily for ease.
She'd heard the end of them, and in no present
Grasp could shake the prying of the words
He'd said about departure that would come
Too soon. That day within the Temple touched
All days, and was not lost or covered with
Forgetfulness, and in the after days,
It waited like some fixed, unblinking star
That would not fade. Her dreams were made of it,
And mornings rose beneath it, still unfading.
Time was not a slowed pace generous
For squandering, and careless in the gift
Of more. The days were jewels, hard and small,
For her to hold; the sun was lapidist,
Incising dawns and cutting at the dark,
And she was one who looked to see the facets
Shining preciously, and one who knew
Days must be gathered up and held and set,
And never lost.

The heart's urge is enough
For this, the merely human hungering

That is as common as the burn of tears,
And little loves that beat across our own
Adventure can admit us in some kin
To what was hers, and warm us to some strong
Appraisal of her days. We'd not be sightless
Nor a stranger if we'd look within
Our next poor loneliness, or watch the aches
That wait before its fall. Too many count
Against farewells, too many turn from them
To let hers be the single urgency.
We've known this watch, this clearness, this too lucid
Essence drawn across the gift of time,
And if we know no more, and never reach
Her purer measure and the constancy
That was as breath, or pulses, or the need
For prayer, and keep beneath our own awareness
Flawed withdrawals, and our prudent, small
Retreats from pain, and are content with some
Alloy and trace that is not love, we hold
Enough that we be made initiate,
And may discover reasons real enough
For aching, and so valid that if none
Were mounted further, we should know her days
Were gathered, and her Nazareth was fleet.

But there was more. We say it when we speak
The younger word and name her full of grace.
This too is hunger, and a clarity
That we can share and can perceive not fully
As she knew, but only in the part
We hold, and stand adorned in distantly.
She was not tempered with the lags of earth.
She was not soiled to dimness in the dusts

That we have raised. We've heard it so. This soul
Was full of grace, with no capacities
Unfilled, and no retentions, where the lights
Caught instant answers, and all askings flared
So swiftly to response, the breath-wide shadow
Of delay is struck to nothingness,
Too gross to move between what God would grant,
And she would seek. Aye, we have read it so.
It has been said of her, full, full of grace.
Who only wanted Him. Who had no sight
Beyond, nor other wish, nor glance to less
Horizon, who was hungered of a single
Need, and who was sharpened to one clear
And edged perception that He moved, *He* moved
So near to her. This is her Nazareth.
She was not lulled by all the days of it
To soft satiety. She was not swathed,
Nor filled, nor resting in a smoothed complaisance.
She was eagerness, and sight and truth,
Who woke each day and *knew she looked on God.*
That He was resident. Was near. Was near,
That He was conscious of her and revealed
His eyes. That she was *seeing, seeing* Him!

This is a strong wine quenching in the soul
An inner thirst. This is her daily Tabor,
Quiet, long, unfrightened, where His garments
Yet were bearing only stains of toil,
And on His face were only summer suns.
This is the moment Thomas knew, made long
And clearer with no need of offered wounds.
She need not die as Lazarus to hark
To Him. She heard. She heard His voice as jars

Of water will await Him for command
To wine. This is the hunger and the bliss
That build the cloisters and the lonely cells,
And in some faint affinity to her
And to her sight, look after Him and count
The solitude, the purging and the pain
Too kind a prelude for His consciousness.
All the Carmels are at Nazareth,
The convents and the corridors of saints,
The hopes of mystics, and the clear, unhindered
Moments when the stark walls keep the breath
Of all attainment and of gratitude.
So quietly she held it all, and held
Much more than all, so sweetly in the run
Of days, unstraining, gentle, unperceived,
Across His growing, quiet in their wait
For evening to end, above a cup
And smiling when He stopped to deeply drink
Of waters she had cooled, and when He'd turned
A path and as she watched Him, waved salute
And came to her.

O, she had known that space
May be a thief of many things, that it
May snatch at nearness and at ease and take
All sight and sound and leave the days as some
Poor emptied purse, but she had also known
The one thing, and the soul's one clear delight
That distance may not touch and may not steal.
She had remembered that there are no plains,
Nor leagues, nor seas with God, and no refusals.
She would not be separate from Him,
Nor left, nor lost, nor shut away in dark

Denials. He is always here, and here,
And when the instant struck and she could watch
Him turning on a road that would not end
Again across her gate, she knew He would
Not then be gone. And further knew the tasks
That had embraced some shepherds and some kings,
Must soon increase and widen till the world
Is Nazareth. And she'd be in the world.
She knew of this, and made consideration
In her heart. And if the pain was dimmed,
And thereby was assuaged to less of ache,
It was not healed and only hid itself
So deep it could be sometimes like a secret
Buried that might seem to be not there.
But it was not destroyed, and all the inner
Sureness could not make it otherwise
Than that she saw Him now, and heard, and one
Day would not see. This strong immediate,
This plainer gift, this reaching of a hand
That found His brow so easily, this clearance
Of the spirit's thickets and the need
For search, this tangible and certain grant
That was not now of striving nor of hope,
Nor of remembered grace, this would be held
And offered up by her to what is Willed,
This would be turned aside and lost. There was
No blotting out of that. It was a truth.
And in the hidden aftertime when He
Would be among them with the parables,
And wandering across the hills to seek
Among the upturned faces, this remaining,
Deeper, purer loneliness will be
Above Him for a nimbus and a sign,

And following, the unseen skeins of it
Shall stream across the skies and down the airs,
And will be scarved above her distant breast
That will be source, and rise, and end of it.

But now, and for a longer time than she
Might dare to wish, there is no sorrowing,
Or turning yet through barren distances
And no abandoned house, and no held tears.
And only in a town, a home is made
That moved to gentle words, and in the good
Repeated rounds of easy dailyness,
Of labors done, of laundering, of sleep,
And meals, and neighbors, and the slam of doors,
Of little plans and smiles and worryings,
They held an old peace settled in an older
Mold, and in the sameness and the drone
Of Nazareth, found blending, and they were
But seen familiar faces in its ways.

We cannot think that ecstasy, or mark
Of adoration made a strange flame burn
Beneath her eyes. It was her soul that burned
With it in fire that held the sear and beat
Of love within her soul. No swoons, or flights
Of vocal orisons broke through the even
Manner of her breath. Hers was a watch
So steadied, strong and silent, only He
Who knew the depth and breadth of it might know
The certainty. She wove the lyric loves
Of heaven in a woolen thread, and bore
The crying of the seraphim in words.
There was a stature here and strength to hide
Her halos quietly. And if we'd think

Of sorrows and the day, that for the length
Of days might be but one beyond the next,
Or still more near, we must not make inclusion
Of a sombreness and think that tears
Were trembling, and her brow was always pale.
This was a woman with a Son to raise,
Who watched for Him, who planned and labored, made
Her small resources yield their managed good,
Who had a calm word and a sinewed answer
To their needs, who saw Him grow, and marked
His strength beneath the tan of many winds,
And who would seek, for always, after Him.

This length of wait to Cana keeps the first
Of all the closings and a pattern's end
That had been caught and weaving in the years.
The first chord rested here in first of all
The long resolvings, and a man was done
With following of dreams. It is not said
To us he knew no more of roads, nor watched
Again in winter where a star once burned.
We have no word of eyes that came to rest,
But only that his soul had held such strength
That he might stand with her, that he had worked
And wandered, been a guard for her and wall
Against her fears, that he had hewn and builded
Of the timbers and had led them here
And waited for a while, and then we find
No more of him. There is no word of Joseph
After Nazareth, and now his name
That had been uttered for a frequent shield,
And raised so gently with her own, is said
No more. There still are pains to be for her

He might have soothed, and moments when we might
Have thought she'd call to him. But he is absent,
And she does not turn to him again.
We've noted this, and we have felt the fall
Of silence and the fading of his name
As we might feel the sudden loss of one
We'd loved, who'd been for us an uttered voice
Before our need. We've searched for him again,
And have not found, and in a longer wisdom
Pondering, so deep across the years,
We've learned some syllables of prayer that speak
In answer to this silence, since it speaks
Of him, of Joseph, and it asks that death
Might be for us a moment sweet as his
Was sweet, that we might know a not too far
Resemblance of the love surrounding him,
Who died here on a day, and in a house
At Nazareth.

Joseph was a man
Who'd marked a single measure on his days,
More true than lines he'd drawn for guiding tools.
And if it brought him now an end to life,
He found no blurs, nor griefs, nor any sad
Confusions. He had asked but one assurance,
And had held so strong an eagerness
That whisperings and dreams had been enough
To send him striding once beneath a dawn
To find her and to give his life and lift
His strength for her. He had not needed more
To find a road to Egypt, and to fend
The fears off and the hunger that was near.
And he had earned this roof that sheltered them.

And for a long day he had watched Him grow
In wisdom and in age, and he had seen
The young hands harden to the boards and come
To competence. Joseph thought of that
So many times and smiled at it; He'd grown
Now, He was strong, and had the stride of strength,
And he had seen her confidence and poise
When He had answered with some service she
Had asked. It was a long way since the stall
Beneath the stars, and now there was no need
To carry Him, nor search with her through streets,
And when the pain came and he knew that dreams
And voices speaking out were now not needed
To instruct him in his part, and breath
Was slower pain to him that dragged the sharp
Air piercing to his breast, he must have sought
For Him? And with his eyes, looked calmly, deeply
Into His? And saw Him standing there?
Aye, Joseph knew. He was a man who *lived*
Because he knew. And now he felt His hand
And knew His hand that closed upon his own!

And Mary. Once or twice he must have said
Her name. And she had answered him and gave
Again his name back, that he'd hear of her.
She was not weeping, or the tears that came
Were not the tears of weeping, and his name
Was love for him that she was saying only
In his name. There were no other words,
And only prayers and tears could carry it
To him who knew how blessed and held and wreathed
He was, and what his name said, and the sound
Of her. She'd seen these creases come to track

Across his brow the signs of care. She'd known
A softer line above his temple, moist
Now in the stabs of pain, and she'd remembered
How he'd searched, and what he'd said to her,
And how he'd looked when lanes were dark, and empty
Sheds were all he had to give.

And then
She was not thinking, and the long past lost
Its separate and clear eventfulness,
And sank within her deep beyond the held
Distinctions of a time that now had gone,
Yet was so near, it was a moment whole
Within her heart that looked to him and watched,
And watched, and did not turn away, and watched
With no more words, or thoughts, or any search
For thoughts, and lifting in her love, became
Her gesture softly that had soothed and touched
Him there.

Death is a long time, not in time,
But in the waiting, in the vigils kept,
Intense. It is a watch that stares observance
Of the faint, tremendous fluttering
Of eyelids and the struggled breath that breaks
Again impossibly from out a wait,
Drawn long enough to be a hundred deaths.
And when it comes, death may be paler light
That casts a calm, released nobility.

And they were two who watched his misted eyes
In love so great it reached across the ebbs

Of strength and gave itself to him for ease,
And for a warmer knowledge this was part
Of life that he was keeping now, as once
He'd knelt and on a night yet clear to him,
Had taken in his arms a Child.

And when
His spent breath sighed away and stillness came,
Suffusing on his face a look of longer
Stillness, she was watching him, and waited
In an ache of waiting for a sign
Of further wait. There were no more of signs,
And deep within her, turning like a thread
Of sound that twisted upward from a further
Depth, a certainty was winding, winding,
Stronger, wider, winding, till it whirled
And broke in inner thunder, and she *knew!*
She knew that he had died. Joseph . . . Joseph!
Who had come . . . but only sobbing now
Too deep and real, and shaken for the mute
Withholding, and her head was bent to him
In blessed tears.

She felt His Presence then
Who was so near, and found His hand so strong
In closing on her arm. And she had turned
To Him, and with a softer sob and older
Yearning, reached to Him and sought to give
Him comfort in return. To Him, to Him
Who wept for Joseph here as she was weeping.
And they paused, and in a little while
Looked down on him, and gently stooped to him
And kissed his hair.

Joseph was a man
Who'd marked a single measure on his life
More true than lines he'd drawn for guiding tools.

* * * *

Afterward her days had newer sadness
Veined in them and new maturity
Had need to rise and strengthen in her heart
That was alone now in remembering
Her Bethlehem, and watched alone with all
His childhood gone, save only as she held
It dreaming lonely in the dawns that woke
No other heart to look beyond with her
To common memories. She could not speak
With only smiles for language caught complete
And adequate, nor with a glance, raise meanings
In an old scene shared again. She was
Alone, and found that she must learn to turn
Away from sudden listening, and curb
Her half expecting wait for steps across
A door, and be less instinct in the count
Of threads, and work against a quick and inner
Way she had of pausing in decisions
Till she'd heard his word. And in the lines
That imperceptibly had set more certain
On her face and fadeless, and in hands
That folded in her lap too tiredly,
Was loss of him made clear beyond her grief,
And told more plainly than the easy fall
Of tears. The earth will not regain such time

For it is ended now, and other names
Will not be Joseph's name, nor keep again
The refuge and the sharing and the seal
Of spirit's ease. She will not find return.
And Nazareth that yet is Nazareth,
Is not the whole of Nazareth, and will
Not be.

The months that mounted and the after
Years had strengths for her, inseparate
From time and granted of its slow repeating
Course against the severed end that must
Be soon. He still was near. She had not thought
A stronger will or calmer wait for pain
Could be than what was centred in her prayers
Since she had heard of roads that He must seek.
But He was near. He moved beneath her roof,
And still was hers for longer gift and blessed
Renewal. He'd not gone and had not hid
From her in any distance or in tasks
She might not seek. And that was strength, and growth,
And storing, more, much more than she had asked
Or hoped, or would have prayed to find, had she
Regarded only ease; and if increase
Could be, her total love had grown upon
These days until the width and spread of it
Stood tides within her moving that had lifted
Life and all of loneliness to Him,
And on its slow, immeasurable, silent
Press, had borne her to a calm, unfathomed
And secure, that shall not be destroyed,
And where His face was, and responding peace.

A word that had been drifting on the endless
Speech of roadsides came to Nazareth.
A man was preaching in a desert place.
They said he wore the skins of beasts and gave
The gaunt advice of penances, and some
Had gone across the stones and found a fire
Within his eyes, and listening, she marked
Responding, and a restlessness in Him.

She did not speak of it, and in the house
That had been Joseph's, felt the nearer rise
Of eagerness that lay between His heart
And hers, and caught the trembling of an old
Compulsion strong in Him again, and gave
Across the silence, hungered prayers that met
His hunger in the one plea that was His.
There were no fears, nor hopes, nor soft demands
For a hearth unbroken still, or for the doors
Kept longer latched. She wove no silken bond
For Him, or cast reluctance like a skein
To hold Him near, and when He watched the hills,
And when the night came folding on Him yet,
So distant in His reveries of time,
She had remembered out of all the swelling
Past that once she'd given Him to arms
That long were empty. Then she did not think
Of swords that Simeon had told, but only
How his sighs had held such sweet content.

And now there might be many Simeons.

The first brief words had multiplied to more.
They said again a desert prophet spoke

To Israel. There were reports of him
To pass from mouth to mouth, and news to tell
That spread among the hills and touched again
The house of Nazareth. He was baptizing.
He had preached of time, of haste, of sin,
He spoke to them about deliverance.
And then she heard them say he cried of One
Who stood within their midst and Whom they did
Not know!

The airs were heavy with a portent
Stirring as a child turns in a womb,
As if an inner prayer had piled to weight
Beyond endurance and was yielding, moving
To a wide relief. She sensed fulfillment,
And the urge of held, tremendous loves,
And heard again of John, and words of John
Set burning in the desert place. He spoke
Of Him, the latchet of whose shoe he was
Not worth enough to loose!

Of all the silence
Drawn about her, this is deepest silence,
Strong against a world that chatters up
Before it and recedes, our little noises
Hushed and held abashed for reverence.
This is departure. This is gift of Him
She makes and only silence holds the deep
Farewells. It is not even said He went
From her, and only that He came to John.

What was the day, or night, or hidden moment
When she walked with Him up to the last

Edge of her earth and saw Him pass beyond?
What were the words she heard, and spoke, or were
There words? What fell to her? What did she give
In gesture or in tears, or in the long
Look sealed across the last place visible
Of Him? What tore her then? Or was there quiet,
And a muted exaltation singing
Peace? This is another Bethlehem.
She wraps Him in His childhood's years, and turning,
Lonely, lays Him in her heart.

Some steps
Retrace a path that ended in a door.
It was her door. She'd closed it many times,
And knew it and the walls beyond and all
The corners and the sills and where the light
Would strike when she would reach and open it.
She knew where He would be, and Joseph, where . . .

It was a door she came to. And the years.

XIII

MANY voices and the easy laughter
Breaking, swirled around her in a room
That held the flow of movement and the wishes
Of a wedding feast, and in the midst
Of ardent kindnesses, and jests, and gifts,
And old communions felt again, and warm
Beneath the moment and the words, she moved,
And was a deeper kindness, soft, subdued,
And busied with an unobtrusive care
That this might be an ample banqueting.
She was a woman quieter than most
At Cana, who had given to the new
Betrothed a gentler gladness, and her smiled
Embrace and hope for them had held a sweeter
Sound, and now she was among the rest
With tasks to do. It had not been the end
Of living after He had gone from her.
She had not clung to grief, or made of loss
A dark confinement, or forbade the beat
And brush of life to touch her pitied pains.
She was not nurse to sorrowing, but walked
The worn ways in a steadied tread, and met
Again the faces she had known, and spoke
To them, and said that it was true He'd gone
Away, and said in answer she would not
Be gone. And then could offer them from out
The surface of attention some concern
That touched upon their own cares and the small

Swift pleasantries. She stood again where she
Was looked for and expected; she was here,
And there, and held the common interest
In daily speech, and she had sought no sad
Withdrawal, and alone, became no more
Than what they'd always found observable.
And long days turning and the inner lag
And twist and ache of hours lay hid where all
Things had been hid, and where the listening
And wait, and hark for Him among the very
Stirs of blowing air, could not be guessed
Or marked beyond a loneliness that clothed
Her, falling like a shawl that always had
Been hers.

The weeks had moved away to more
Than weeks, and she had drifted on the ebb
Of them, and could not measure time that was
Not time but absence, more than she could hold
That it was time when He was near. She could
Have had no sudden news returned about
Judean crowds that gathered at a stream
Where hopes were high. She had not known the Voice
That spoke to call Him Son, and she'd not seen
The Dove; nor heard of deserts afterward,
Nor scorn that sought not bread. She was alone,
And only found the word they find who are
Alone, that is not memory so much
As present listening without the need
For other aid than what lies in the past
And is too clear. And Nazareth had seen
Her usual and old accustomed rounds
Proceeding in unaltered ways that were

As they had ever been, and had no sign
Of her or any sadness other than
A Son had gone away.

And so a claim
From Cana could include her in the plans
Made for a wedding. They would send to her
And ask that she be there, and she would go
To them and be awaited in the good
Expectancy that did not pause to think
It could be otherwise than that she'd be
Among them now. Some friends, perhaps, who'd loved
Her from the long ago. Or kin of hers
She'd visited and had within her own
House on occasion when they'd come the few
Miles up the road. Cana was not far.
And whosoever'd asked, she'd gone to them,
And brought an eagerness unreticent
For all her grief and gave of charity
That still could find another's joy held out
A valid urging in her world.

The cloth
Was laid and women were exchanging judgments,
And regarding touches that might seem
To bring a last completion, and the talk
Ran on in pleasant ease. She must have stood
Among them, aproned, quiet, keeping such
Anticipation as the moment held
For one who was a part of festival,
And who had put her hand to all the tasks
Of it. She was a figure, competent,
Accepted, who awaited with the rest

For further word, when someone said that more
Had come to keep the wedding feast. She turned,
And over many heads, she saw Him smiling.

He was thin, and worn, she saw that first!
How drawn He was, and thin, as if His strength
Had met a laboring that drained of Him!
As if He'd fasted, and His eyes were yet
Too bright with hungering. The sun had burned
Him. He was tanned with it and taut above
His cheekbones, and she saw the hollows dark
Where pain had passed, and then she saw He had
Not come alone.

He was surrounded. Men
She did not know were close to Him, and He
Was speaking on, and she could see they were
No sudden strangers but had held a bond
In Him and many words had gone before,
And they were close to Him, and listened now
Against confusion, and had come here since
He'd said they were to come. Her thought then ran
To Nazareth. He'd gone there. He'd returned.
From out the distant place, and after days
Of walking on the lonely paths, He'd come
Again. And she had not been there! She'd not
Been there! The caught breath stifled in her throat,
And for a moment, she was not alive
Except to all the emptiness she'd left
For Him to come to, and the search He'd made.
O, John says this, young John who saw her first
Across these boards at Cana and remembered
That it was the third day, and she'd gone

There for a wedding feast. He writes of it
As if she'd been a goal they had been seeking,
And had only found when they had gone
Beyond her Nazareth and come to Cana
After her. And it was there she was,
At this place, not some elsewhere, but at this
Place, at this Cana that he'd lifted up
His eyes, and down a cluttered room, had found
Her shining suddenly for him to see
Forever. He retells it so. He speaks
It as a man speaks who can lose the time
And frame and circumstance of her no more
Than he can lose the gladness and the thrust
Of what he found. The look of her, the words,
The attitudes, of how *He* loved her so,
The turn of things, the consequence and prelude,
What she said, and how she stood and bowed
Is cut intense in him, and he cannot
Forget. He writes of Cana. John, young John
Has told us this, who is a white flame caught
Now in the flare of whiter flame that will
Be cast around him always, and which he
Will know for first strength of virginity
That takes of her, remains, and ministers
So close to her. But now she does not find
Young John, nor Andrew, Philip, nor the rest.
They yet were nameless, and were only crowding
Figures that she did not know and could
Not see for seeing Him. So drawn He was.
So wearied, and His eyes that for so long
Had been the pain beneath her dreaming, met
Her own, and asked, once more, for Nazareth.
Across the bobs of movement and the murmurs,

Over laughs of welcome, instantly,
She read the hunger sunken in His eyes.
It cried to her. It reached within to lost
Depths in her soul, and lifted up the surge
Of answer. He had need of her. He'd come
Again. He'd come to her, and home. And she
Had not been near to break the sandals' straps,
And bathe His feet of all the roads. She'd not
Been near, and now there was this outer thing
Of festival to close on her. This house
He'd come to, this was not her own, nor these
Her silences that dwelt in it for Him.
She could not shut away the earth and run
To Him; it was not hers to put behind
Her rising sounds and names that made the sounds,
To pull the doors in, close her eyes to all
The pale futilities that were not He.
She could not loose the tears, nor let the cries
Come that were surging, breaking on the impulse
Of her heart, and she was only glad
As mothers may be thought to be, and shared
Her gladness with the rest in reticence
That told no more than that He was a Son
Returned Who had been long away. And then
She kissed Him. And the voices raised again
Around her in the murmurs of a feast
Made gayer now that He had come to it,
And questions in her eyes were still unsaid,
And they had only seen a moment's quiet
Deeply claiming her, and that her hand
Had reached to Him and trembled on the line
Across His brow.

They gave Him invitation,
Warm and laughing, they were pleased in Him,
And spread more places and made eager welcome
For the few who'd come with Him along
The way. They'd feast here, and the steward hailed
The cups for them and spoke aloud their names
Most heartily, and called for more of wine,
And said they were most merry and that feasting
Should begin.

She was apart from Him.
The quickened need for serving held her far.
And they had given her some bowls to take,
And jars to fill, and spoke in words and broke
Away attention from her lingering,
And from the distance to His place to nearer
Centres where her hands moved for a moment
Undirected, and where suddenly
There was a need for her to be concerned
At trifles far from Him and not of Him,
And here beyond Him where she was, and where
She was not seeing save by eyes that were
But eyes, and where she heard and did not hear,
And where the thoughts ran on, of Him, of Him . . .
Turning, turning, Him . . . His look of pain . . .
His weariness . . . of what He'd borne . . . of what
He still must bear . . . His cloak . . . the exaltation
Lifting in Him . . . hidden . . . hidden . . . visions
He had found, of where He'd been, and these . . .
These five who came with Him, His look of pain . . .
His weariness . . . His face . . .

The men reclined
At table spoke across to Him. And He
Replied and gave His own wish back above
The couches in a word of good intent
For him who was the bridegroom, and they spoke
Again, and He was turning to the rest
And drank of wine.

She still could catch the sound
Of miracle His voice wove clear for her
Among the rest, and over them she listened
For the rise and fall and threading skein
Of it that had no need for meaning other
Than its sound to be a speech for her,
So rich the duller rumbles down the room
Were left unspoken, and she only heard
Of Him.

The hush of her, her wait and search
For portents and responses, for the shine
Of stars again, for attitudes and signs
Of kingdom, for unfoldings, past beginning,
Why He had returned, were held within
An inner pondering that had been life
To her so long it was its own strength now,
And rose in her as unbetrayed as prayers.
And she could feel the edge of other ache
That only came because there had been cradles
Once, and He Who was so tall, was once
A Child.

The feast had latitudes of ease
For her, and some permissions she might take

In serving when she moved to Him and watched
More closely and might lift to speak to Him.
But she was near at times, and she had seen
The drawn lines that the desert cut, and read
The imminence of labor and the press
Of fiercer pains beneath the faint absorptions
Passing in the shadows of His eyes.
She knew His dreams, who had been watching them
Since Nazareth, and knew the loss in Him
That she was ended, and that now no more
Her peace lay waiting for His heart; and heard
Again their speech of John who had been once
A prophet for these men who came with Him.
They spoke of John, and others heard of him,
And listened in a long sobriety
That stilled above the jesting. She was near
Enough to feel the pregnancy that hid
Beneath the moment. Time, and breath, and air
Had harked beneath the sense of it, and swollen,
Weighed, impending issues slowed beneath
The surface of their words. Aye, she was near
Enough to feel the sombre urge of currents
Moving, and to say a low word now
To Him, and touch His hand, and could pass by
Again unnoticed to the serving place
And be more silent there. And smile again,
And add to gaiety a gentle measure
In her own observance, and a soft
Remark about the feasting.

She was swift
In seeing wants, and turned the steward's glance
To them, and spoke to waiters quietly,

And gave them of the trays, and hastened them.
The hospitalities were guarded here,
And opened larders spoke the kindly share
The bridegroom offered of the joy that came
To him. He'd pledged the honor of his house
For her, his bride. It was a day for that,
And they were eager for the warm progression
Of the banqueting, and nodded down
The good assembly of their friends, and looked
To them. And they were pleased. And confident
Of all providing.

She had caught a word
And question whispering among the women.
Of the wine they asked, was there a store
Of wine beyond the cruses drained along
The table? Was there wine? So many came
To keep the feast. The wine was failing. They . . .

It's plain to us. The welcome of the wine
Had failed. Some words of counted stocks and small
Provision were to force a blushing entrance
In the speech of him who'd claimed a bride,
And asked his friends to come rejoice with him.
She knew, whose hands had scraped her own bins out,
And hoarded crusts, she knew what need might be
For calculation, and what lack had masked
Itself in plans, and she had seen the care
That sorted measures judged enough for feasting.
She was there to watch them, and could feel
Too quickly what the issue was that hid
Beneath the questions; she would know of that,
And we have been alert to catch the swift

Identity that rose to take the threats
Upon her own heart, and that moved her near
To Him to say in whispers that they had
No wine. We have not needed counseling
To follow where her feet led, and to find
Her hastening among the guests to Him,
As to an instant strength, and wanting only
This small crisis and this little pain
To plead with Him. We've noted how she brought
Him simple words and was content to speak
No more than that there was a need, and she
Was anxious. We have seen her good concern,
Nor shall eternity demand of us
We find much other here than she was kind.

But there is more. There are more depths to Cana.
What is this she came to ask of Him?
What stirred within her mind? What did she ask?
The wine had failed, and therefore she beseeched
Some word of sympathy for them, some gracious
Covering of imminent and swift
Embarrassment? Or did she ask for more?

John, young John, whose life had met her here,
And who was witness, writes for us He answered
With refusal. That He asked what cause . . .
He asked of her what cause! . . . had they to be
Concerned with wine. He turned away whatever
Plea it was He knew she'd made to Him.
And John has not forgotten what the sound
Was in the wording He had willed to use.

My hour is not yet come.

There are more depths to feel at Cana. We
Have trembled here and faltered, but we've seen
Her confidence, her poise, the almost regal
Calm that dared to lift beyond His uttered
Answer, and could hold against reluctance.
We have marked the ease, the simple sureness
Deep beyond the need for more adornment
Or repeating in her plea to Him,
As if among these guests and with the gown
Of poverty wrapped sweet and close around
Her, calmly, with the years up-piled, standing
Here, and prideless in the fall of truth,
She knew that she was mother to a Son.

Aye, we have kept this vision in our eyes
Through all the aves we have sped to her.
This certainty, this undismayed and dear
Assurance that could rest upon her face
Against His answer and be strong in her.
This we have seen, and we shall not soon lose
The consequence so vivid then to John,
How easily she turned again to them.

His mother saith to the waiters: Whatsoever he shall say to you, do ye.

But what request had gone to Him of her
That is unsaid upon her words, and cause
Enough to lift in Him the ancient thunders
Rumbling at the edge of Israel's skies?

My hour is not yet come.

What is she asking and is sure of now
Beyond recall? What moved beneath recorded
Speech, communicate, and passed between
So deeply it is silence reaching on
To silence and responding utterly?

Some listless men have gone to fill with water
Jugs that stand before His place, and she
Is waiting, calmly, quietly for them.
This is her hour come, and through our long
Reflecting prayers that rise beyond the full
Accomplishment beginning here, we've known
It so. We've seen these moments beating up
To Cana's table fall on her and fall
For lustre burnishing all given suns
Of shining that had clothed her, to more shining
Suns that will be ever hers. We have
Not lost among the sight of kindness, honor
Set here for eternal diadem.
This instant now of plain divinity
Has moved upon her word, and only comes
In summons to her call. She stands precursor
Here. Her lips have spoken in announcement.
She has pointed Him away to Tabor,
And unwound the roads His feet will take
Until they move from this place to the flags
Of Pilate's floor. This is the gathering
Of crowds, the pain, the glory, the defeat,
The long inaugural of Calvary,
And she has summoned it. More now than sweet
Persuading innocence that holds a Child
And sings for joy of Him, more now than woman

With a woman's heart to be a place
For swords. She is the sum of all the advents
Crying in the past for Him to be,
The first among her fathers, and the last
Voice speaking of the hundred prophet tongues
That told of Him. She is the star again!

Once, long ago, she had been searching Him
Through days of dark, and she had found Him seated
In the Temple's porch among the old.
And she had asked Him then, and issues trembling
On the air had paused, and He had come
Obedient to wait at Nazareth.
And now she's brought to Him another plea.
We have not heard it. It is left unsaid,
And only breathes in silence after speech
Of wine. Nor have we heard Him answering.
But she heard. There are words to say she heard.

Whatsoever he shall say to you, do ye.

So men are pouring water to the brims
Of stone, and she is waiting, quietly.

And in her heart? A gift again. More strong
Than when she made it first beneath the sigh
Of angels in the past of Bethlehem.
He was a Child that tumbled at her door.
He was a Child. She had not known that hers
Would be the plea to send Him to a sooner
Hour, and turn Him down from Nazareth.
But He had given that. This was her word
That He was answering. And she was glad?

The quiet is too deeply strong for that,
And is too sure. She stands beyond the tears
That Simeon might once have seen in her.
And knowing, she is sharer in His Will.

The jars were filled and John might glance from her
To judge that water brimmed them to the bulk
Of two or three good measures, and he turned
Again to follow where she watched for Him.
She did not speak, but waited for His word.

And Jesus saith to them: Draw out now, and carry to the chief steward of the feast. And they carried it.

The murmurs and the feasting's cordial tones
Had not died down, nor dwindled for the little
Space of silence that had come upon
A few who were surrounded in the wider
Gaiety. They had not paused in laughter,
Nor remarked the sudden isle of quiet
That their voices broke against in waves
Of unconcern. It was a wedding day,
And they were feasting in the joy of it.
And if a hush had fallen on the servers,
And an awe had slowed them, and their eyes
Were staring at the wine, and in their hands
The cups were trembling that they dipped in it,
They could not notice. Wine is for the drinking,
And the toasts renewed in warm, more hearty
Humors at the rarer vintage passed
To them, and out above the new increase
Their murmurs made, some running words are clear.
The steward sipped his new replenished cup,

And in a voice of wise urbanity
And some regard, he laughed to the bridegroom's smile:

Every man at first setteth forth good wine, and when men have well drank, then that which is worse.

He sipped again and lifted up his cup:

But thou hast kept the good wine until now.

She watched the whispering that spread along
The room, and saw them turn to Him, and taste
Again, and turn to Him once more, and held
It in the widened beating of her prayers
That on their hearts had fallen reverence
That did not fear, and that they moved to Him.
This was a kindly thing they'd seen, as kind
As new creation and the earth are kind;
And awe, and wondering, and urge of stronger
Impulse on their minds could not deny
The gentleness as manifest as glory
And before it in His way. And she
Who was among them, whom they'd known for all
The years of life and looked to, who was one
Of them, she was His mother. Standing so,
She was His mother. And they could not fear.

He rose then, and the murmurs broke to loud
Quick shouting of a clear acclaim. His name
Was on their lips for praise. The feast had ended,
And the cloths were left half pulled across
The tables in their haste to crowd around
Him at the threshold and to follow Him.

He moved away. He was returning down
A road again, and many walked beside
Him for a space and ran ahead of Him,
And only turned away when He had spoken
Of Capharnaum.

And in the dust,
And walking near to Him, she saw His eyes
Held no denial she might read, nor sign
That she must pause and watch Him go, as once
Before He'd turned away from Nazareth.
She was included, she might be with Him,
And for a little, be among these men
He'd gathered. They were hushed now, muted, stilled,
With newer bonds across their hearts and surer
Cords to bind them strongly for His own.
They'd seen. They'd seen the wonder of the wine.
She watched them there. These men who came with
Him,
And who were turning now up to His face
To look on Him. She knew them. They were shepherds
And they hastened up a pathway through
The night. And she had shown them Him!

XIV

THE line is written of Capharnaum
That He and she were there "not many days":
And whether John who wrote it only meant
To say they hurried on and nothing more
Than that, or whether he permitted here
Beneath his scripture some brief, lingered tone
Of wistfulness that would have been in her
Accounting, had she summed this time, or all
Of time, we need not judge. It is enough
It seems declared that she had known an end
Of Him again, and that the pain of going
Was as sharp and hidden as the thrusts
Of old departure, and had not been changed
Or lessened, and was not now different.
The same sword entered here that she had kept
In other wounds, and this was still the same
Held hurt that she could not put by nor lose
So long as distance was a thing between,
And not some vague assumption that she knew
In reason lay beyond Him for a world
That was not He. That had not changed nor come
To be a new, less quickened pain, and whether
Waiting now would be the last and never
End, or if across expectant space
A day would rise that might be soon tomorrow
Bringing Him again, she knew that more,
Much more, was here than had been in the past.
There was a change. The very hills and stars

Had altered in the sense of it, and these
Were not the same dawns that had been before.
He *had* gone on to Cana. He had answered
Her, and wine had poured along a table
Bare of wine. They'd seen that. They had risen
Then, and all the nights they still might sleep
Could not persuade them they had dreamed. It was
Not now as if He had not stopped a moment
At a bridegroom's feast and never could be.
It was done. He'd crossed a threshold, made
A sign and moved beyond it, new among
The sons of men. Cana was behind
Him now forever, and the fall of it
Set Him declared and designate. His Father's
Business had begun, and in whatever
Long revealing might be made across
The hills where He had gone, deep joy might be,
Or sorrow, or the thousand names for anguish,
But there never could be now return.

She'd watched Him go away and had not asked
To follow Him, and only held within
The willed heart of remaining loneliness
How swiftly these few days had cast the light
About Him strongly, how a few brief hours,
The words and gestures found in them, had raised
Him now apart and laid on Him another
Garment than the homespun she had made
For Him, and thought again, how much was told
Already, and how much could be so soon
A story told. A while ago He'd come
And searched a room for her and He had found
Her, and the hunger rested in His eyes.

But they'd not spoken much, and at the feast
There'd been much more of laughter than of prayer,
And none who could have said they'd see the end
Of any more than wedding festival,
Nor more beginning than another home.
And now He'd gone up to Jerusalem.
And she was left here, and the airs had stirred
Behind Him and had stilled again of breaths
Remembered of creation. He had called,
And on His voice the earth had heard an accent
Falling that had sounded to the voids
And summoned them to filled obedience.
O, Cana named Him! He was walking now
With emptied cups behind Him for the end
Of eras and with light upon His face,
Unheld, and clear, and visible, to break
The darkness in the sight of waited dawn.

Known things can be a fire within the mind,
And in the mind a feeding root of fire.
A certainty, a knowledge can be flame,
Be sear, be burning in the soul to pulse
In throbbed, repeated spread until the flamed
Devouring moves along the last recesses
And the soul is fire. She knew that He
Had gone across the hills to speak to men.
That this was *His* tread on the earth now finding
Roads. That this was *He* whose worlds had waited,
And Who had now gone to them. She'd known
Him. For the long months He had hid in her,
And she had known Him then. And in the years
Of silence, she had lifted adoration,

Lonely, deep and steadied in her eyes.
But now He'd gone, and in these moments now
Above her and around her, in this time
That fell, in these quick minutes falling, breaking,
Other eyes could look upon Him plain,
Be filled with Him, and see Him, find Him, now!
This was the hour! It was advancing. Now!
Across the skies. Beyond those lifted hills,
There where He'd gone, His worlds were finding Him!
And that was fire and burn within the mind
Enough for flaming.

She had waited this
Too long to find that any press or pain
Or joy was stranger, or was otherwise
Than what she'd known among a thousand dreams.
She'd lived this day and learned the feel of it
Before it had been nearer than the far
Maturity that hovers as a promise
On a Child. She was not lost to new
Surprises. This was time that had been hid
Too deep among the heart's expectancies
To rise now of a mold that mere release
Had altered much. She recognized this sun.
This wind she'd always known had been a secret
Waiting only to be whispered from
The places of His stay. She'd known its touch
Would feel so on her cheek, and she had known
What prayers would be returned upon the wind
For Him and be so strong and filled and sure
That He might know she'd not been left to weep
In loneliness.

But she had not forelearned,
Nor sensed by any promises, the sharp
Taste stinging in this present, nor the whetted
Tang that cleared immediates had raised,
Nor could have told how edged and pungent time
Is, over mused anticipated time.
That waits us till awareness freed of futures
And of searchings is so bared and quickened
To the held shape and the plan of things,
We find the vague perceivings we had guessed
Were only dreams of dreams and were not real.
She could not think she would be watching leaves
Upon a tree to mark if they had turned
And trembled to the way that He had gone.
Nor thought that shade and dust and common faces
Lifted in the old accustomed sameness,
Could be rimmed in new and altered aspect,
Be so charged with tiny, strong, intense
Assurances. It was not prelude now,
Nor looking to the margin of a day
That might be soon, but was not in this day.
This was His hour, and earth was drinking now
Its draught of hope held of the ancient years.
She'd known this was to be, and known the full
Accompaniment of prayers she'd give for Him
To follow in His wake and be around
Him silently. But that was in a hope
She held, and was conjecture only, faint
And dimmed and vague among the long surmisings.
This was real, with outlines, places, time,
Directions, names and fall of circumstance
Already clear, and she'd not thought how deeper
In her heart the shafts might strike than she

Had measured, nor how wide the sounds might search
Among her mined resources, nor had guessed
There were such veins and lodes in her untouched,
And yielding up a richer gift than she
Had known. Yet it was so. These pleadings drawn
Beyond her estimate of strength and given
Him, were prayers and ardors not suspected,
Till impelled and driven in the hard
Force of a present undelayed, she bade
Them be, and still insatiate and strong,
Had summoned them above the spended last,
And made demand on them that they be His.
These moments were an artery of prayer,
A pulse that could not pause nor rest nor hold
Its throb, and could not end except that life
End, and the heart be drained of it. She gave
Them that His Name be lifted up and over
Him be love. She gave them for the paths
His feet were finding, that they might be thronged
And dense behind Him, and that after Him,
There be no other paths. Her silences,
And where she moved now, and the places blessed
In her, became for Him a far and hidden
Home where He was closed and roofed and warmed,
And where a handmaid looked to Him, and served
Him in His need.

We do not think of that,
That one voice cried in Israel to plead
For Him, that He was not alone, nor left
Forsaken in His restless way, that silent,
Hidden, hardly known, unnamed save once
Or twice in brief allusion, unperceived,

She waited in the cloisters of the hills,
And kneeling made Him conquests in her prayers.
We've seen her loneliness and guessed at pain
That might be made of time and barbed in it.
We cannot lose the wheels of fear that turned
Unreasoned in her mind to leave her shaken,
Trembling, in the hard unheld return.
We've known that, and we've known anxiety
And search for word and sign might be in her.
But we've not summed the full remembrance left
To us for stronger treasure till we've marked
What dignity, and part, and worth she had
Who was so distant, and who was so near.

It may be, beggars came to Him because
Of her, and were not frightened since she asked
For them. It may have been a prayer of hers
That made a blind man cry beneath a gate.
What weariness was eased in Him, what words
Found good ground waiting, what brief gesture caught
Attentior since she prayed? How many thieves
Observed Him kindly on a narrow street
Before He spoke to one upon a hill?
What is the measure that her pleading made
In favor of a woman at a well,
Or through a prudence Nicodemus had?
How much of hunger will she raise within
A throng who'll hear of Bread? He is to speak
Of prayer and harvests whitened in the field,
And is to say to them that laborers
Must come of God and be beseeched of God.
And He is Laborer: and from what distance,
In what force and urgency are hers

The prayers that gave Him sheaves among the fields?
We do not think of that. Yet she was there,
Somewhere, somewhere, real and living, near
To Him, or far from Him among her own,
Or strangers, somewhere, conscious of His Name
Upon their speech, a woman, actual,
And whole, who bore upon her arms the weight
Of Him remembered, who was like to Him
In brow, and voice, and contour of His face,
Who knew that He was walking on this land;
And dare we judge her heart was only waiting
Now and paused within her silence stilled
Of prayer? She who merely in her own
Existence held a part in Him? So schooled
In pondering, so exquisite and swift
To meanings?

There is much of shadow left
About her way. The fall of light is His,
And she would only seek for deeper shade.
Yet this is clear to us, these were His days,
As all days of the past had been His days,
And parables, and signs, and all the words,
The long persuadings and the sharp and salted
Speech of Him, the lures, the angers, loves
And scorns, were spoken of an utter Wisdom,
But they were not said alone.

She could
Have had no whisper of the roads His feet
Were finding, nor of time, nor of intended
Plans, or end, or hope, or change in them,

And save in what her mind caught of its own
Perceptions, she'd not known how far He was,
Or near, or when it would be hers to come
To Him. She had no inner visions other
Than the store of all the past that only
Looked to Bethlehem, and lingered here
With her along the little lanes and stones
Of Nazareth. She had returned to this
Sweet place of quiet, we may guess that now,
Since it was there unbroken and still held
A room with doors and cots and woven things
That still were hers, and still were tangible
And real upon the earth and made a house
That was her own. She was not yet uprooted,
Nor beyond the claim of older days,
Nor would have thought there could be easy reasons
For another place for her than here.
And we may judge that when the distance opened,
And the winding road was bringing Him
Again through mists of time and far horizons
To her Nazareth, she waited Him,
And watched Him turning with the sun behind
His head.

He came not unattended. Words
Preceded Him, and in these last days, rumors
Had been running up from Cana telling
He'd returned and stood again with them,
That men were moved in Him, and had been caught
By urgency that roused them, that He'd made
A sign beyond the wine they had remembered:
He had healed a man, a ruler's son,
They said, who had been dying and who lived!

The wind that was His name already moved
Among the hills, and men already swayed
To it and felt it was a wind that would
Be rising on the land. And when He came
To Nazareth, she did not find it sudden
Revelation that He should be near.

She waited on a road and watched for Him.

And did not see Him as it had been hers
To see Him in the long days gathered here,
And strewn along these streets to be a deep
And ended past. He was new now, new,
And almost stranger. There was that about
The look of Him to make it so. His aspect,
Some compelling ardor or assumption
Strong in Him, His stride, the altered, eager
Search that fingered faces in His glance,
The knowing men had knelt to Him, that He
Had let His voice fall tugging at their minds
In more than speech, and something, clear and set
Beyond her made her see Him now as other
Than a Son Whose least look she had learned.
He had been ministering. Aye, that was it.
He had gone out to distances, to time,
He'd stepped beyond possession, hers or His,
Or Nazareth's. He was the seeking Christ!

She saw that. And could see and find it only
What had not been once forgotten since
She breathed consent and gave Him way of her,
Yet stronger now and shaped to Him and clear
And visible, like light to clothe Him, light

So inward, fallen, undenied, she knew
That if He walked upon this road, He was
Not now returned. The old perceivings still
Were there, the dearnesses, the looks, the lifts
Of manner, form and face and tone of Him.
They were not lost. These too were of forever,
And were sealed in her. But there was more,
So much she would not let the eager cry
Of hunger break beyond her heart to call
To Him, nor give above her silences
Another welcome than was held and ordered
To His name. She would not ask Him now,
Nor think to ask, as once before she'd asked
Within His Father's house. A first had claimed
Him, and He'd gone to it and more than need,
Or smile, or fairness, or response in Him,
She saw that resting on Him as a vestment
He had lifted up to Him and worn.

* * * *

Within their synagogue, a little group
Had felt the word He uttered, and had turned
To it as if warm life had touched them from
The dried scroll at His hand. He had unfolded
To a prophecy Isaias made
Of Him, and in the weighted after stillness,
Poised again the sounding of His voice:

This day is fulfilled this scripture in your ears.

Since shepherds came, she had not known such soaring
Lightness curving up through her to sing

Away the misted dark and make her glad
And young with joy again. They'd heard Him, heard
Him,
They had heard Him! He had spoken out
To Nazareth, and they had found a grace
Upon His words, and she could see a bright,
New wonder starting in their eyes, and find
The answering beneath their speech that echoed
Him. It was a task for her to give
Attention here or there, or to one murmur
More than others when such eager flood
Of them held running joy for her to follow
Quickly, and to seize lest in some fresh
Release, she lose a gladder implication
Or a further sign. They were so filled
With Him, so moved, so near to all the hopes
She'd spun and woven for a distant sight
Of these good days. She heard them speak of Joseph?
Was this Joseph's son whom they had known
And worked with? Was this He Whom they had seen
Take up the tools upon His father's bench,
That spoke now in this accent of renown
That they had heard, and were so glad they were
Alive to hear? And was He not their own?
She marked their word of Joseph, and remembered
Him, or did not find so much remembrance,
As a pause his name gave, and a warm
Back turning of her love that had not gone
From her and did not need remembering.

But it was there, a sudden tie they spoke,
A bond more closely uttered she could hear
Again and feel that He was close, and this

Was Nazareth. For all His words, He had
A home here. They would name Him hers, and Joseph's,
And be unafraid. He stood so real,
So of the earth and kindred to them all.
God's way with men has been to take men's way.
O, not the thunders and the lifted gates!

And for another evening, she found
Him walking quietly beneath her stars.

She might have guessed He'd speak to Nazareth.

The broader movement and the quickened pace
Of days begins now, and the wind that was
His name will grow beyond the farthest hills
Until the urge and sound and flowing feel
Of Him is all about them, on their faces,
In their ears, beating in their sleep,
And met again at waking, on their fields,
Their shores, their roadsides, blowing down their streets,
And up to all the shuttered synagogues
To stir the prayer shawls and to swing the lamps
That hung along their roofs; unquieted,
Persisting, stronger, blowing as a wind
That grows, that may not now be turned away,
Nor left evaded, nor be made to end.
After Nazareth, He is a Man
Who walks the roads out from Capharnaum,
And will not rest, save in His chosen place
Of secret prayer, and in the little circles
That the poor will make Him of their love.

She did not follow Him. We guess that too,
And certain only of designs and manners

Visible within the broader pattern,
Dare to piece this in, and say that it
Is ordered to the known way of her will,
And is not alien to what has been
Disclosed of her. She could not cling to Him
In tears, nor give Him other than a freedom
Glad for roads and towns, nor seek to be
About His feet and slow them to her needs.
We do not read of her among the women
Called to Him. It is not written down
She stood at Naim, nor listened when His words
Fell from the mountain like a dew that still
Is fresh and clear and cool upon the fevered
Earth. She is not scurrying along
A beach, nor waiting at the edge of crowds
For Him to notice her. She does not count
Disciples, linger in the wake of lepers
Who had cried to Him. She does not watch
Beyond the frowns of Pharisee, nor move
With Him upon a Sabbath in the field
Of corn. He is alone. And she is hid,
Alone. So silent. Silent and apart
And far from Him.

* * * *

But one brief interval
Is told us like a sudden light that flares
Around her in the dark before it fades.
She is a woman then who stands on tiptoe,
Straining over many heads for sight
Of Him, and holds upon her face a bared

Pain of anxiety lest there be need.
They'd brought her here by telling of the fury
Of His way. His brethren, they who held
A tie in Him, and her, and were around
Her, said He wasted at Capharnaum
What strength He had, or sense, or such a prudence
That might be the better gathered up
Again as once they'd known Him on a day
Less wild than this. He was beside Himself,
They'd heard that said, and He'd not eaten now
For such a length of time, it could arouse
Concern if other causes were not firmer
And more prominent within their speech
For seeking Him.

But if she'd hurried on
And come with them, it was to speak to Him
Of nearness only, and to give Him word
Of strength and look on Him, and in the look,
To find that He had seen, and be assured
Again He knew, and that no more had come
To trouble Him than what was less than long
Maternal thoughts could conjure and could not
Quite lose, nor keep forever held beneath
A reasoning. She did not fear for Him,
It was not that, but she could be with Him
A moment, only see Him, speak to Him,
Be warmer comfort, give Him of herself
And leave Him with an ease beneath His heart.
She could be there.

And so this rarer sight
Is manifest, and Mark records it starkly

On the page he's left us out of Peter's
Memory. She stands among a throng
That presses Him. She comes so close to Him
She hears again His voice and finds again
The urging of response and of a need
Awakened utterly, until the lost
Days far from Him and spent and cold beneath
Accepted silence are destroyed again,
And fall away before the warm resurgence
Given her of life, and in the sound
That, rising, comes to her. It is enough.
She would not ask for more distinguished meanings
Than this cadence carried on the hushed
Air, stilled to Him. She would not seek to know
Of any more than that His voice was raised
Within this house, and she was near the door
And could be gathered in the sound of Him.

They moved her inward, urging, crowding in,
And let it then be said that she was His,
And they were His, and that they sought for Him.
She heard Him now more plainly. Some debate
Engaged Him. He was speaking on with strength,
And held them to Him in an awe that gave
Reflection He had made a bold avowal
That had shaken them. He'd found a hard
Refusal. He had met and held a foe
They'd known of, and they'd seen Him pit alone
Against the suave assurance they had feared.

He was alone, she sensed that. He stood lonely,
And it had not been too well with Him.
She had not missed the fringed phylacteries

That failed to tremble in an ecstasy
At what He said. These were not all His friends.
But she was near. Because she was His mother,
These too general and vague reportings
Struck in her, and could not be assuaged
Until she came to Him. And now she stood
Here, tiptoe, and she saw Him. Harried. Lonely.

And they say to him: Behold thy mother and thy brethren without seek for thee. And answering them he said: Who is my mother and my brethren? And looking round about on them who sat about him, he saith: Behold my mother and my brethren. For whosoever shall do the will of God, he is my brother, and my sister and mother.

The inference is left us that He turned
Away then, and continued on with speech
That had endured this small parenthesis,
But was resumed again, oblivious
Of all save that He had a more considered
And a longer word to tell to them.
He had been interrupted, but His voice
Broke strong again, and they were listening.

She felt attention tighten, and around
Her shoulders strained and pushed ahead, and little
Shuffles moved them closer in. He'd had
Enough of pause. They had distracted Him
A moment with the word of her. He'd learned
That she was near, that she was near and stood
So, just beyond the crowd's edge and had come
To Him, and like a man who hewed to larger

Business, He'd dismissed her and gone on,
Forgetting her.

She'd heard Him. She had heard
These sentences and knew them. They were hers.
She'd known they were to be, and that they'd fall
For her and were to be her own against
A world of men that might be free in them,
But could not own them, nor the pain in them
As she would own. This is her day's completion.
This is night, fulfillment. This is thrusted
Sword that had been entered to the wound,
The hurt, the pain of now, the bared pain, stark
And stripped of more delay and faced to her.
She'd held this hour and tried in prophecy
The sharpened edge of it. Had she not heard
That one day He'd be gone and would be gone
Without her? That she'd keep no part, and He
No plan, nor place, nor reference for her?
He'd asked her once did she not know of this!

She'd grown since then, in strength, for that was long
Ago when she was young, and she'd not had
The years to ponder then, nor words of His
To turn in hid foreboding of a way
That would be hers. She was not now untutored,
Unprepared, with inner strength unlearned
And tentative, and standing here, she should
Not now be quivering by any anguish
Keener than the years had taught to her.
She should have known of this, and in her heart
She had perceived His words were only meanings

Risen up to hard and present outlines
Out of dreams. But she'd not grown so far,
Nor come to such acceptance, she was lost
To all except a bloodless revery
That said, "How true," and gave a little sigh
And turned away.

She was a woman here,
A woman who had seen a long love close
To her; who heard a sound that was an end
Awaited, and who knew that no appeal
Or cry or staggering of hers could stay
This certainty, or turn again the sound
Until it still was only time expected
And not time begun. She was a life
That came to withering within a word,
That felt a sudden silence fall and widen
Till the brief endurance through the length
Of only one quick breathing, seemed a space
That had no edge, beginning, nor progression,
And would have no end. She was a woman
Who was made bereft, who felt a pall
Close suddenly upon a warmth that had
Been hers against a hundred lesser pains,
And now was gone. And she'd not grown beyond
The reach of *that* denial, nor advanced
By any prayer or virtue to a sphere
Where loss of Him could be another loss
Than what was hers to bear and what was real.
She knew no time that was pretended time.
We must not mistranslate the dark scars healed
Above the wounds. She'd heard the word He spoke.
She stood here lonely at Capharnaum,

And when her hand had fallen from her brow,
And strove no more to give a shade against
The sun that she might see, and find Him there,
And when she moved away and left Him speaking
On, and did not pause, nor turn, nor waver,
She had gone one distance more, and found
Almost her last maturity.

O, she
Might take with her this accolade of all
Distinction He had uttered, and might bear
It simply and unfeigned for honor to
Her soul. O, she might know this too was hers,
This bond in Him He'd said was only made
Of free obedience, this taller crown
That was the wearing of a Will. She'd kept
God's Will. Since long ago when first her word
Had fallen to His seeking, and before,
She had been gift to Him, full gift, and kingdom
Given Him, and bannered in a glad
Surrendering. She knew that. She could find
The praise hid in His words and take away
The deeper recognition He had made,
And hold to that, and in a swift skill learned
Of pondering and many prayers, add more
Assent and emphasis and grant Him quick
Agreements now. She did not find He'd spoken
Of rejection or that she was scorned.
If ties were only fastened by a will
That serves His Will, then she might be the first
Of all, and strongest bound, and in this still
Be His, and even by the sterner judgment,
Still be mother. More than that. She carried

In her heart His certainties, the pain,
The need, the disregarded loneliness,
And all the love He had, and knew they were
The sure reflections of her own.

But she
Had turned away, and out of sanctity,
Or prayer, or meditation, could arise
No truth reversing that, to make it less
Than fact or less than pain, and where she moved
Was not where He was visible, or where
He'd speak again and she would hear, or where
She'd find Him waiting. She had turned away.
He was behind her. It was ended now.

The sun's glare was a blade that pressed against
Her eyes. Some figures crossed like thinning shadows
And were gone. She did not look to them,
Nor search them for a sign, nor seek to find
In them more than the nameless shadows moving.
They were gone. She could remember now
How she had searched once in the glare and sought
For Him. He had been lost. She could remember.
He'd been lost. And there had been a word
To think on that the pain was what it was
To be. She could remember that. She'd not
Forgotten. But she made no searching now.
This was not promise. This was time, was *time,*
He'd turned away.

* * * *

There is but small accounting
Afterward of Nazareth, and Luke
Has left us with but brief, too sudden tale
Of swift uprising violence that makes
Us gasp for her. She may have been a cry
Here lost in harsh confusion and a part
Of it. She may have seen Him, watched Him, staring
At the wild rejection and at bitter
Fists thrust to His face and clenched to Him.
She may have been at Nazareth when He
Returned. We do not know, so many things
We do not know, but where upon the earth
Was other shelter, where was home, since now
She might not be with Him along a road?
He had returned, and stood again before
Their synagogue. They'd asked Him why He healed
Not in their midst, and how He dared to heal?
They'd known Him. They had seen Him at a bench,
And could give off the names of all His tribe,
And now He made them sermons, and had brought
His famous wonders to another town!
And He had answered them and spoken truth
Of unbelief, and said again a truth
That turned the skin back from their smarting pride.

And they rose up and thrust him out of the city: and they brought him to the brow of the hill, whereon their city was built, that they might cast him down headlong.

And she was there? Among the dusts of it,
The running feet, the shouting? With her hands
Pressed to her mouth, and frightened, staring up
The way they hurried Him? And knowing cliffs

Were there and stones, and seeing fevers lusting
For Him broken, limp upon the stones?
So strong for numbers, brave, indignant, loud
In righteousness that was contagion freeing
Hate? She saw them? She was there to cry
To Him? To call Him Son? To gather in
The blasphemies and wipe them clean along
The white upoffered sanctities her soul
Held out to Him?

A place upon a hillside
Close to Nazareth is named for her,
And on it now an altar has been raised,
And it is said to those who come to pray,
They kneel upon the very earth where she
Was standing. This is hers, her place, they say,
A long tradition makes it so. She stood
Here, held with fear and fixed upon a spot
That still remembers what the cry was when
She saw they did not pause, nor mean to pause
When they should reach the edge. This is her place,
This ground, and whether memory is here,
And truth, or only yearning and a need
For more of certainty than may be gained
Among the sparse words left to trace her way,
We're sure of this: it would have been a place
Too far from Him for Him to see her tears,
But not so far in distance or in pain,
She was not near to Him. She would not run
Among them, wild with protest, snatching sleeves
And pushing at their breasts and stumbling, crying,
In the tumult and the dust. She'd be
Here, motionless. And when He turned to them,

And with no word, or gesture, or defence,
More than His eyes that looked to them and held
Them so, and walked among them, calm and sure,
And free since now He willed that He be free,
She'd still be moveless; and would only watch
Him turning on a narrow path He'd learned
In kinder years, and down a little street,
And past a further hill, she'd watch Him go,
To leave forever, this, her Nazareth.

* * * *

Almost since she could remember, time
Had been intense in her, so urged, and limned
In strong importances, so pressed to crisis,
So minute and drawn across her heart
For inner portent, visible and cut
Beyond all loss in blurred anonymous
Forgetting, she could find that what time gave
Now of fulfillment and the risen, swift,
New meanings of His way were only what
She'd always known. These wider days, when He
Was raising issues and demanding faith,
When speech of Him was dinning in the Councils,
And the roads were live with poor, when winds
Were stilled, and listening had come again
To ears that had been dead to sound, when He
Was moving, threading in the fields, and bold
To twelve in prophecy of pain and kingdoms;
When He sought for challenge, spoke above
The Temple, laid a claim to life, and startled
Them to Him with love; these days that came,

And that she learned of from afar, told only
Old significance that she had found
Already in the silence, and had kept
Within the years. He'd come to other birth,
And she who'd held Him longer, could not take
A new awareness since they saw what she
Had known of and had not put by or lost
Since time began. And like all time before,
These weeks and months had mounted to a past
So swiftly, she could search among events
For Cana, and could find it seemed as distant
And as young as shepherds were, and far
Away as songs that they had told beneath
The night. How long ago since He had gone
From her? How many years since He had rested
In her single kingdom, and had had
No ministers to go before Him, nor
A throng to follow Him until they'd faint
Along the way? How long since He had said
His first revealing word, and come to them?
How old was John, and Peter, and the rest
Whose names ran now within her and became
Like names of friends she'd always known, and spoke
In thought so warmly when she thought of Him?
How old was she, how old, in loneliness
And prayer? She could have named no years for that,
And had she paused computing, would have said
He had been always taken, and there was
No measure left that could reduce to length
An age that had not been compiled of time.

She was so tired. Wearied now, and tired,
And the strengths that had not flagged and had

Not faltered in the long toils given her
In all the past and in the poverty,
Had need now of a stricter will and need
Of summoning, and she could find they were
Not endless, and that she was drained and wearied,
And the burdens were not held with hands,
Nor were fatigues unweighted in the ease
Of sleep.

We need not think that she was always
Distant, and that never in the years
She came to Him. There still were feasts to keep
Before Jerusalem and she could go,
And move among the women and be near.
And minister with them. And they would know
Her and be reverent and hushed to her.
And she could speak to Him, O, speak to Him
For moments, for the moments speak to Him!
Discover homes He knew, and friends, and loves
That gave to Him and were impelled and instant
In the eager spending, strong in comfort,
And a refuge He might find, and she
Might find, against the labors and the pain.
They must have known her there at Bethany.
And of her silence learned of Him and learned
Of silence. There are other Marys named
In long remembrance who would know what grace
She was, and what He praised once when He said
She was more blessèd in the will she gave
Than in the breasts that fed His infancy.
But they would know that it was she who bore
Him, and it was on her arms that His head
Had lain, and they'd be glad she had come near,

And they would look to her. She'd smiled to James,
But noted that it was young John who stayed
So close to Him. There is not need to think
That she was always stranger to the eyes
That only saw since He had stooped to give
Them sight, or that she was not one more gift
They might now see. She could have known the sun
That shone on Lazarus again, and watched
Him walking, and among the rumors, sensed
How much affront he was, and that the years
Had grown; and all the words that had been said,
The illness healed upon the Sabbath, sins
Forgiven, all the refutations made
Too plain, and answering hosannahs lifted
Over Him were mounting, meeting, piling
In a swollen cloud that leaned above
Him, big with dark, and that He moved now under
Nearer thundering.

She could be surer
Than the rest, and even at a distance
Wide as many hills, could not be dulled,
Nor slowed in deep perceivings of the moods
That gathered now around Him and the hidden
Murmurings. She was too swift in strong
Impression, she had lived too long upon
The earth with waiting to be dulled to Him,
And what was near to Him, and out beyond
All forms of words and tones and slower lingered
Sadness on His voice, she could be sure
That time was ripening, and that an hour
Neared.

He had been definite, and they
Had had His counsel, and the warning words.
They should be strengthened. They should know of
Him.
But even had He not so darkly spoken
In the uttered prophecy, they heard
And thought on afterward, she would have known.
There was a sense of old resentment weighed
Upon the air. Too much of brooding stood
Beyond the road and pondered Him. He loved
Too many poor, and they had been too ardent
In their speech of crowns. And He had been
So long among them now, and He had traced
So many patterns in their minds that were
The one same pattern meeting in His name.
She knew. By any call or turn her heart
Made deep within her, she was sure.

And knew
The issues! And in cried commanding strength,
Raised up consent again, and in a last prayer
Made of it desire! She'd given Him.
She had not faltered in the long ago.
She had not looked away or turned her sight
So only that the pain be not denied.
She'd willed this thing for Him. She'd willed Him slain,
That was her will that she had driven on
To be so lost in His that it was His.
She could remember. Simeon had seen
Her eyes and Joseph had been there to be
With her. She could remember. She had not
Forgotten for an instant breathed along

The years that now were gone from her, and now
The hour of total gift was near, and still
She'd not forgotten. She was greyed now, wisps
Of hair that with a gesure she had pushed
Beneath her shawl, were grey, and on her face
The lines of recollection were too plain.
And she was strong, beyond the darkness falling,
Over pain, and need, and over love
She'd given Him. And she was glad in Him.

O, be it done to me. He was her last
Of answers. After Him no more was left,
And she'd be emptied, and the soul could seek
No further full annihilate to add
For more surrendering of more. He was
Her end of giving, and the grant that God
Would have of Him, signed in the opened Side,
Would reach to her, to take as utterly!
And there'd be nothing then, and in *her* heart,
No more to give for more.

XV

DUST was rising and the smell of heat
Hung thick upon the air, and figures seemed
To move grotesquely in the straining orbit
Held within a swollen, dulled confusion.
She could see them. They were moving. Moving.
Down. And up. And circling down again.
Figures like a darkness in the sun.
Some were standing. Many there were standing,
And they did not move, but only swayed
And shuffled back and stood again above
The dust they caused, and in the heat. The waves
Of heat were shimmering along the clear
And windless noon. The waves of heat.

She had
Been pushed. A shoulder, huge, unmindful, struck
Against her heedlessly, nor had it yielded
When she'd staggered and held on a little
To a figure close to her. But now
She stood again, and shut her eyes an instant
To the light, and with a soiled hand wiped
Across her face. That too was soiled, and had
Been streaked where tears had dried. She was not crying
Now, and moved a step again when more
Of surging and of crowding made her move.
The ground here was uneven, and a stone
Bruised through her sandal and the hurt of it
Gave sudden, strange, immense concern for her.

The hurt, and that the ground was so. Uneven.
Hard. She must be cautious. She might stumble
Now. And fall.

A woman there was weeping,
And she watched her sob. That woman there
Was weeping and another near to her
Was weeping, only quietly. She was
Some older, she who wept more quietly,
Her face was older, and she did not lift
Her hands. Her own hands were not lifted up,
And when she bent to look at them and find
Them, movements came again among the crowd,
And murmurs, and a burst of loud commanding
Somewhere, and a clattering of hoofs
That ceased with shouting and a crackled curse.
And she did not remember she had meant
To see her hands, and stared away, and was
Distracted then, and when the crowding stopped,
She found that she had not moved far, and dust
Was dry within her throat, and on her lips,
And she was shivering, as if the heat
Were some enveloping that could not reach
Within to touch the deeper cold that trembled,
And would not be warmed.

Her eyes were dimmed
And stinging, and she saw in forced and long
Minute intenseness that the studs of brass
Upon a soldier's strapping were in patterns.
There. And there. In patterns there. Until
He moved away, and then the sky was free.
A bird was winging. Lonely. Far. Aloof.

She followed it a moment in its calm,
Unhurried order that was strange, now, strange,
Like memory from out a world that once
Had been. She did not will to look, or make
A conscious choice to wonder at its flight
That was the same swift spurning of the earth
That birds had always had, but it was there . . .
And she was seeing it . . . and piecing out
The faint, relieving miracle that it
Could be. Unchanged.

And then she turned too quickly
To a hand that sought her own, and stared,
Unknowing, at a face that looked to hers,
And shivering again, found anguish, tears,
And hiding horror, wide beneath the eyes
Of one who meant to give to her some pitied
Comfort she could not have grasped, or held,
Or recognized within a mind too long
In pain to tell if this were ease, or one
More pain, or one more need to drain a strength
From out her spended store, or only one
More cause for tears. She stared an instant, groping
For an answer, while the fingers clutched
Upon her veils. And then she looked away.

Too much of quiet muffled on the air,
The sound of voices, and she felt the hush
That gathered round her. Ominous. And deep,
And pressing down more weighted than the heat,
And closing her, and seeping in to slowly
Wake awareness, where the tangled noise
Had gone unheard, and had been only distant

Paining, far from her, and only waste
And remnant washing as an edge of sound
Left yet of all the fury and the splitting
Screams that had been swirled about her head
And flinging up since dawn. It was so sighing
Down to silence. They were moveless now,
And heavied in a hot, oppressive quiet
That brought in to her the feel of quivered
Waiting. Held. As if the multiplied
And sweating pores of all about her, stared
To one thing in a common strain intensely.
They were waiting. Solid now in fixed
Absorption centred on a place beyond
Her there. Some time had come, some moment waited,
And the breathing slowed to it, and pulses
Throbbed. Aye. She could feel it. Padded, soft,
And evil silence creeping in the heat
To smother sound. They were not speaking now.
Unnatural and spread, descended silence
Thickened on them, and they were like men
So held before revealing, and afraid,
They dared not see, and dared not name with words
The horror they had climbed a hill to see.
It closed on her, the waiting and the press
Of dread, the fascinate and stirless, single
Staring of their eyes.

Some voices spoke
And answered, and the quiet fell again.
Until a breaking laughter somewhere ripped
And split across the heat in pitched, unloosened
Crying, as a man might scream whose soul
Was feebled unto cruelty and laughed

Obscenely to the sudden sight of wounds.
As if he'd seen a man's flesh skinned from him!

She felt recoiling in the crush and breaths
Retracting, and the stifled sobs around
Her. Then, the after quiet, tightened, trembling
At too much fulfillment, and in wait
For more, and only broken by the sound
Of other movement, definite, and sure
Of what it must accomplish, and intending
With a last efficiency to be
As blunt as orders from a judgment seat.
She was alert now, and her own breath slowed
For listening, and in her breast, the worn
Heart raced to rapid pounding, and the senses
Cleared. Exhaustion turned upon itself,
And inward willed that it be not the end,
But lift again above the squandered loss,
And for her find a new strength, though there be
No strength except demand that there be more.
Her eyes were startled, wide, and glancing, roused
To fear and opened to the fear, and startled.
She had not raised up her head, and fear,
Or certainty, or intuition, pierced
Too swift for reasoning. It was a moment
Only. Silent. Whitened in a clear
Perceiving, conscious utterly.

And then,
The wheeling of the world and time was stopped,
And for a rigid instant came to fixed
Eternity. A sound rang out to silence.
Once. A single sound. Of iron beat

To iron. There was gasping in the crowd,
And little cries caught rising in the breast,
And ended. Then the mounting, breaking ring
Of iron beat again to iron, beating,
Beating, sounding to the air on strokes
Of iron, beating to the skies that filled
And rang and held above the world the iron
Beating down and sounding till no more
Of earth, or life, or memory was left,
But only on the air, the beat of iron,
Iron, sounding, sounding beat of iron.

She was made *alive* in it, responding
In a loosened fury that could leap
To strike away all intervening forms,
And stones, and turmoil, all the skies, if need
Be, till she'd found and reached to Him. O, this
Was fury rising, leaping in her eyes,
Impelled by sound so dominant and beating
In, it was not sound but other being
Come to be alive in her, and throbbing,
Throbbing in her with a whole compulsion
Moved upon her love and driven down
To all maternal instancies. It lifted
Answer, full, unheeding, and beyond
The hold of either guards or strengthlessness.
She'd be with Him. She'd find Him, strain to Him,
To Him Who was her own, and in the sound!
She had no need to fling away exhaustion,
Nor to make command that life be roused
Enough to meet this last of chaos splitting
In a world that long ago had cracked
In pain. This sound, this sound of hammering,

Was all of her, and flaring to a wild
Denial, terribly, she lifted up
Her head, and with a hand to set against
Whatever hells were there, she turned to Him.
An arm had reached across her shoulders. John
Had hold of her. And women stood so close
She moved against him. They had turned to her
She found, and found that she was near. Not far
Away, but near. And then she saw Him there.
She had not moved beyond a step. But He
Was there. She saw Him.

We have grown so used
To looking on a crucifix. We've seen
So many crosses, delicate and cut
In ivory, and holding up the white
Christ placed in all proportion. We have seen
So much of symmetry and carven wood,
And we have come so many times to find
Him in a shrine. We've worn this on our breasts
And clung to it, have gone to sleep beneath
It for a prayer, and waked again. And we
Have known Him crucified. His head is upright,
And He stands upon a solid ledge
With arms extended, and with dignity.
And it is good. Aye, it is good for us
To shape Him thus in meaning, and to leave
The stark remembrance covered in the years,
As once the darkness closed upon a plainer
Sight. We could not bear to see, no more
Than others, older, nearer to His day,
Could bear the naked horror of a cross.
They could not look upon a crucifix

So easily, His first of followers,
They could not look, for in their lifetime, they
Had seen men nailed. Beyond a city's gate,
Along a road, they'd seen them; bodies broken,
Stretched and drawn and taut upon a stake
And crossbar; nailed to it, and reddened, writhing,
Like a raw scar cut against the sky.
They'd seen them, twisted, sinking of their own
Weight pulled upon the nails, with tongues extended,
Heads that swung in torture side to side,
That lifted up and cried for death in babbled
Spurts of sound. They'd seen them. They had seen
Men nailed. This was a death the Romans gave
To slaves. This was a death that held contempt
And pain and shame, all fastened into one
Great spreading gesture, set and bleeding there.
And this was His death, done to Him upon
A hill, and they could not be quick in looking . . .
Even on a sign.

But she was near,
She saw Him. She could see His cross in making.
Full. And plain. So near, her eyes could find
No shield, nor lesser sight, nor any refuge
From the full perceiving, had her love
Been frailer to have searched for it. She saw Him.
Staring. Near enough to fill all need
She had that could be filled, and near enough
To fix in her a locked intensity
Of rigid pain that raised forever lost
And lonely ultimates that only He
Knew, and her sharing heart.

His knees were twisted,
Drawn athwart the body, quivering
Along the black beam laid upon the earth.
He was not still. They held Him, *held* Him there,
Until the long first spasms died, and they
Could tighten cords again and stretch His arm
Down to the hand that was not nailed, and pry
The fingers open. She could see. And then
The sound again! The iron, beating iron,
Iron beating, and the twist and squirm
And shaken answering in all His form
That lay beneath them. He was nailed in hands.
Forever now. Past restoration. Nailed,
And nailed, and nailed. His hands that could not fall,
Nor open. She could see them. Shut in iron,
Useless, shattered in two pegs for hanging
Him.

There was no need for John to hold
Her then. He sensed a calmness come to her,
Like life beginning that had ended once,
But grown again until it was so sure
And strong, it seemed a Will had summoned her,
And she was finding now an hour drawn
Beyond apportioned days and given her
To live because it was her own, and she
Had only lived before in wait for it.
He looked to find her standing, taller, moveless,
Firm. No cries now, and no tears. No lifted
Arms to fend her way to Him. A woman.
Pale. So stilled. How utterly so stilled!

And then a last completing blasphemy
To break His manhood, done to Him to leave
Him less than human and to smash against
A post whatever worth was in Him yet,
Whatever name or dignity He had!
His legs were straightened. They laid hold of Him
And pulled Him to a line and crossed His human
Feet that still were free, and measuring,
And forcing strain and fixity, they nailed
Them, flattened, single on an iron shaft
That they might never be His own again
To use in freedom walking on the ground.

She saw them rise and stand aside to look
On Him. Aye, He was nailed. He should not move
Much from the brace He made against the wood.
They'd set Him well, and He was shod and gloved
With iron on His feet and on His hands
For what remaining time He might endure.
They were assured of that. And one of them
Stooped down to post a writing over Him
That He might keep His claim and keep His crime.

And when they'd moved again as men who'd done
A task, in this impossible, this flared,
This first and staring instant, it was clear
To her. The last design. The fixed, completed
Form, the pattern of His pain. The fact.
The true, the outlined, the accomplished thing
That had been turning in the years beneath
Events since she had been a woman dreaming
That a Child would be. This was the end
Awaited that had come and was the end.

Fulfillment. There, before her, visible
And made. The rigid trinity of hammered
Ending. No returning now. No time
Or places further. She could see, could see
The dark signs lurking in the prophecies,
The threatenings, the pain that in her heart
Had never been so absent she might turn
From it, the fears, the waiting, all impressed
And shaped and certain, bared to her and stark
Upon the definite, relentless wood
That lay in stubborn angles for His cross.

And somewhere, in her, through her, giant wheels
Were grinding, and enormous in the brazen
Rims of light, they turned and were a larger
Round beginning. Worlds had pivoted
As if the earth were straining, and the sun
Had wheeled against the sky and she was now
Absorbed, and stood amid the chaosed swing
Of spheres and spaces where the light was sound,
And sound was light, and where she was who swayed
And held resisting to a thinned, determined
Edge that she should not permit, and willed,
And willed again that she should not permit
To curve away and falling, fail to her.
Violent and inward she was screaming,
Shouting claims against the swirl, and turning
In to force unyielding huge commands
Against impermanence. And slowly then,
She knew her lips were forming careful words,
But of her lips no speech, and she was conscious
She had not been audible. A prayer
Had stood in her for strength and that was strong.

She had not moved. Her hands still clenched together
Whitely. She was there. And if her breathing
Faltered, and the hard endurance now
Had worn away from her poor fall of tears,
Had beaten in to strip all recognized
And human ease, if she were lost, and emptied,
Spent, dissolved, with fragments of her heart
Left bleeding far behind her in a courtyard,
And in places He had pitched and fallen
On His way, if utter disposition
Came, and loss, and on a hill she stood,
Not woman, but a grief; then this remained
To her, one part untaken, undenied,
That was enough that she might hold a name
And keep identity and be here still.
It was a strong consent that she had made,
And watched, and learned, and fortified, and held.
It was a young word uttered long ago
That was old silence now before His cross.
She had no more. No speech. No strength. No life.
She stood here emptied. And she *was* consent.

A sigh as if a wind along a grainfield
Moved on them, and underneath the heat
The hill was murmurous, and crying came,
And shouting broke again, and from afar
More answering. They'd raised Him on His cross.
She knew that. She could feel this swift response,
And knew before her eyes had opened, He
Was hanging in the sky. They saw Him so.
And bore the impact of Him on their souls
Forever. They could see. He was unfurled
For shame, and marked in silhouette above

The world's edge, and they saw Him now as she
Had carried Him within her in a secret
Held behind the beating of her heart.

And now they knew. He was uplifted, taken
From her, like a wound that had been hidden
In the years, all opened now and clear
For full revealing. This was her love here.
She was not absent. He was speech for her
Who never spoke, and sign that she had made
Him sacrifice within her at His birth,
And in Him found her own annihilate
And long obedience. This was the measure
Of her part, her own Gethsemani,
The watching in the nights at Nazareth,
The lonely pain, the depth beneath her eyes,
Her solitude. He was uplifted, flung
Against the sight and fixed immovably.
And she might lift her head and look on Him
As they were looking. She might see Him now.
Above her. Mounted. He was plain upon
His cross.

But only she could find the dark
Remembering, and what had not been once
Forgotten in the years.

She did not turn
Away. The one thing that we know of her
Is this, she did not turn away, nor fail
Before Him for an instant. It is not
Recorded that she wept or asked a pity.
It has not been writ of her she languished,

Crushed and broken, on the drawing length
Of hours when He stared above their heads,
And felt His warm blood spurting at the nails.
She stood beside His cross. John tells us that.
She stood, and spoke no word. And He could find
Her there, unflinching, statured by the long
Preparing, grown to this, and strong enough
To meet His last need and to wear her last
Tremendous majesty. She was His mother.
What she'd given Him was broken now,
And scourged, and spiked upon a beam; and soon
He'd be bereft of Bethlehem, and she
Would see her life fade out of Him, and all
Her giving move to darkness and an end.
He was her birth, but now no angels came,
Nor shepherds climbed to find Him at her hands.
They'd gone away. But she'd not gone away.
She still was His. To bear Him unto death.
This was not time as she had waited Him,
And felt Him move within her as a burden
Quickening to nearer infancy,
To lift her soul to awe and make of time
But sheltered song and quiet virgin prayer.
She was not trembling now in fragile gladness,
Waiting life and dreaming to a day
When she might hold Him breathing at her breast.
He hung there, over her, outstretched, and stiffened
Streaked in running red, and terrible
For wounds. His feet were held and agonies
Of torsion moving down His body, ended
Helplessly. And she was waiting Him.
O, not the limpid song and eager praise,
O, not for cries that living should be His:

She was a woman, cryless, wrapped in time
That in this dark expectancy would give
Him to His death.

And this was not a night
Of silver stars hushed all about a cave
Where Joseph's footfall and his presence made
A sweeter loneliness, and she was watching
Over Him upon the straw. This was
A day that glared in unrelenting light,
A hill with sweating crowds, a place that smelled
And wavered in the heat, and where He'd come
With timbers on His back to keep a tryst
That was His own, and hers. And she was here.
A figure lost and unregarded, one
Among a multitude, and muted, lost,
But here! O, here at this acceptance, here
At Golgotha. She did not turn away.

She is madonna to His death, and now
She looks to find Him here, this Son she bore.

Her palms curled inward, seeking for the nails
That might not be in them, and asking pain
She might not hold, and on her feet, a plea
For thrusted iron ached and spread within
A wholeness that was yearning unrelieved.
Her arms cried out for bracketing along
The wood that strained Him. She would take this pain,
This brace, this agony, she'd be His heart.
There was not ever sadness in His eyes,
Or lonely striving, never hunger, thirst,
Or any tear that she would not accept

And bear for Him in all the ended days,
Nor any need, and could there now be run
Or race or fired forking pain along
His flesh she'd not have taken eagerly
In full surrender, finding it a gladness
And relief? O, that had been too easy
Joy, too generous and rich exchange
To wear the wounds for Him. She'd be His head
To bleed beneath the thorns and ask aloud
For longer moments she might keep them hers:
Except that in her heart she would not choose
This lesser gift of love, and found again
It was her chosen part to only stand
In silence, seeing Him, to be so strong
She could endure, not her wounds, but His own,
That she could bear His cross that was not hers.

And in another side of mystery
Made one in her, the exquisite and endless
Knowing held, that He was God! She saw
The spittle wet upon His face, the bruise
Still dark where they had struck Him; she could find
His tattered knees, and marked the soil and streak
Of dirt upon Him, left there from the reeling
Moment when He'd sprawled along the road.
She saw the scorn, the slime of all degrading,
The contempt, the loathsomeness of Him.
She heard them laughing at His twisted feet,
And quarreling about a robe they'd stripped
From Him since they had dug Him past the use
Or need of it. And calmly, certainly,
In simple knowledge as a mind might see
Its thought, she knew that He was very God.

She knew Him. Conscious of its need and single
In direction, still her soul could lift
To Him. Beyond the lacerated love
That took to her each tremor, felt her own
The length of this inflexible unyielding
Wood, beyond dismay, untouched, and past
Disheveling of pain, she held the one
Awareness and the swift response that fills
Eternity with Him. She stood here strong,
And was an adoration at His feet.
He lacked not tribute, nor an incensed honor
Given Him. Around Him here was more
Than scorn. The earth was not all saturate
And steeped in evil. She was standing here,
A whiteness circled to the dark, and sweet
For Him. She was a silence hid among
The shouts, a prayer, a sum to overweigh
Rejection, she was faithfulness, and watch,
And praise, and with a steadied love enough
To heal the kiss of Judas on His cheek.
The sun, the hills, the winds were not alone
And uncompanioned. She was here. She knew
His Name. She'd not denied or left unguessed,
Or unremembered Him Who was a figure
Stretched upon a beam. And when His eyes
Should clear to gaze at distances, and trace
The long horizons in until they wound
About Him, and were tightened to the small
Enclosure where the shadows of His arms
Were limits and a kingdom's edge, He'd find
Her here, unbroken, waiting, and His life
Could end as He'd accepted it in far
Beginnings once beneath the stars. Her face

Was turned to Him, and on her face was love,
And adoration, held beyond the reach
Of tears, and stronger than the gift that angels
Pray they might attain, and faithful, bring
To Him.

So long she had been separate
From where His presence kept a closer blessing
On the earth. She'd been removed from Him.
She had not followed where her total hunger
Might be eased, and she could be so near
As to be comforted with only sight
Of Him, and only with the sound of words.
She'd been apart, and He had gone beyond
To walk His dangers and the lonely tread
Of truth. He'd asked a solitude of her.
And was it that she might not see Him scorned?
Was that a part of what His will had been,
A trace within His motive, that she'd not
Be witness to betrayal, see the snares
Set cunningly, and find Him in dishonor
With the poor? But she was near Him now,
When He was lashed, and raw, with thorns upon
His head and lifted on a cross to drain.
And was it only one more agony
For Him she should be here? Was she a further
Pain, an exquisite and hidden aching
Added to the nails and pressed to Him
For deeper sorrow they might not have given
Him, nor could have thought might be devised
Beyond the measure He possessed? Would absence
Be for Him a grateful ease and stronger

Manifest of love? Should she have held
To secrecy and served Him by denials
Of her need, and found a greater gift
To Him in seeking not to make a gift?

But this was hers, this cross upon the hill.
He had not sheltered her from pain, nor ever
Asked she not be free to know an anguish.
She had learned that. He had not been fretful
Nor concerned to throw around her soft
Protections guarding her against a share
In Him. He'd spoken truth to her. He'd not
Been reticent. Nor sparing. He'd not held
Her unadmitted to the full acceptance.
Never. She had heard what Simeon
Could say, and at the moment when she'd found
The Child that had been lost, He'd not consoled
Her in a gentle paraphrase of futures
Eased away from what the days should be.
And He'd not softened any loneliness
When Nazareth was ended. She was free
To sorrow, unwithheld, she could be eager,
Fierce, insatiate, for this was hers
To take, her own, and by a long inclusion
Granted her, she'd known she need not ever
Turn from grief. Of all the spreading earth,
This was the one place she might stand with Him.
She could be near. He'd not deny her now.
He'd not forbid she come here. This was hers,
Her life, her dignity, her choice, the essence
Of her heart's significance. She bore
The right to be here, she could penetrate

To this, this small and inner concentrate
Of anguish. She could stand here. This was hers.
And He would only look, expecting her.

A sense of things begun, of final things
That had been long awaited, poised above
The moments and had fixed them, and had come
To take away the feel of any sequence
And progression, and it seemed as if
The fragments of a dark mosaic, falling,
Fitted to a final plan, and now
There was no movement more, but only set
Accomplishment, that she must ever see.
She knew no time, nor past, nor other life,
Nor could have said He'd hung there for but one
Eternity, or whether that had passed
And He'd been bleeding at His hands for more
Than she had names to utter or the strength
To find beneath the long enduring pain.
They'd nailed Him that He might not walk to them
Again, nor make His gestures in their sight.
She saw the outlined meaning in His form.
They'd made Him helpless. They had done with Him.

And Jesus said: Father, forgive them, for they know not what they do.

She'd heard His voice. Amid the risen tumult
She had heard. And it was He Who spoke.
His voice had fallen. These were words she heard.
His words. Like sounds of blessing, like relief,
Like ease in pain. She'd heard them. She had seen
His lips in faintest movement, and had taken

From His lips the sound that fell to her,
And had forgotten earth, and need, and all
Existence, and all life until His words
Had ended, and His lips were mute. He'd spoken.
She had heard Him, and the sounds that rose
And shouted after Him were only silence,
And she listened, listened, listened, still
Within her to the words that held in her.
And she'd not lose them. This was utterance
To take for fabulous and last increase
In wealth she had; these were a fallen few
Additions come for her to gather in
And count and guard and hoard among the rest
Of treasure. This was new and unexpected
Gift, a precious, sudden raining down
Of sound to close within the harkened soul
Of her to hear forever. It is Luke
Who tells these words, and we can only find
Them on the page that he has penned. They are
Not elsewhere. We'll not find them in accounts
Of John or Mark or Matthew. It is Luke
Who tells of them and does he write from her
Remembering? Is this her sign, her accent
Left to us? Is this her fruit of pain,
A memory cut deep in her she brings
In single telling since she paid the price
Of anguish and was near enough to hear?
She's saved this word, and from the place of sorrow,
From her own place, has returned to give
It unto Luke that he might put it down
Beside his intimate and granted speech
Of Bethlehem? Is this her rescued gift
That we might know she heard forgiveness uttered

To the snarling hill? It would be such
She would remember. This could come from her,
And be a detail she would not have lost
Among the pains. This would be fixed within
Her memory, and if He spoke it softly
Once, or if He pleaded in a prayer
To make a longer dialogue against
Their hatred, she would hear. It was the first
Descending of His voice. She'd hear. She'd hear.

And find He was unchanged and had not met
Defeat and was unvanquished by the nails.
She had not feared that He'd be altered now,
And crushed beyond His inner strength to hold
His heart His own. She had not thought He'd lose
The dominance and sovereignty that made
Him master and would choose for Him His own
Way past the wounds. She'd known He'd not be broken.
Yet the sound of Him, the very word
That came could give assurance. She was strong
Now, she was strong in Him, enough to look
Away, and let her glance, like slow, embracing
Blessing, move across all forms and bring
Them inward to her pity and her love.
She saw them, gazing upward, hard, distorted
In the lust that spat upon His feet.
These men who stood, whose faces she could *see!*

Vah, thou that destroyest the temple of God and in three days dost rebuild it: save thy own self: if thou be the Son of God, come down from the cross. In like manner also the chief priests with the scribes and ancients mocking, said: He saved others: himself he cannot save: if he be the king of Israel, let him now come down from the cross, and we will believe him.

And in her there was echoed but consent,
And this His prayer. Aye, she was strong in Him.
So strong that she could turn to mark their hate
And gather them not in to bitter scorn,
But in to love, to pity answering
As He had answered, and with nothing more.

She looked again to find Him darkening.
The wounds were thicker at His hands and old
In bleeding, and like fruit too long beneath
The sun, His bruises had been turning dark,
And flies were at His head, and He had sagged.
As if a weight had pulled upon His shoulders,
And He'd ceased to strain. He was a man
Who hung upon the sinews of His arms
And did not rise, nor turn, nor fall, but only
Hung, enduring time, and time, and pain.
He hung in pain, unmoving in the clear
Essential hold of it that was like air
Above Him and around Him, pressing, inward,
Constant, near and unrelieved, and still.
She saw Him in His agony, the small
Unconscious flicking of His tongue to wet
His lips, the eyelids, patient, weary, closed
Against the light, the unprotesting wait
Of Him, the gentleness that even now
The savage spiking and the twisted, long
Distortion could not break and could not change,
Or bring to other aspect, or defeat.

His willingness had reached to her and struck
Within her by the measure that she knew
Of majesty, and if there could be grades,
Or peaks, or climaxed moments in her love
For Him, she had achieved such in her heart
That beat to almost ceasing at the sight
Of unrebellion, that He'd bear His pain.
She knew too much for only grief to be
In her. We must not think she did not see
Nobility, and size, and grandeur, all
The victories upmounted in submission
And in taken tasks, we must not think
She looked on Him as other than a man
Who was a man, and therefore had a choice
And freedom in Him and Who'd knelt beneath
Some olive trees and groaned, and asked an aid.
She knew Him. He was hers. He was a man
Who hung there, and her look to Him could hold
A pride, and sorrow could be veined in joy,
And in the deep retracing and retraced
Complexities, and in the run of deep
And inner thought, she could be glad that He
Was He, and find it good He was not other
Than He was, and that in name and form
And in His selfness, it was He Who must
Be as He was, since it was true, He was.

A new voice crossed her mind's intensity,
And turned in it a new attention given
Suddenly to one who did not speak
What all the rest had grown so shrill in speaking.
She had noted him before and pitied
Him for agony that was his own.

She'd seen him with his cross and followed him,
And dimly had observed he was not scourged,
Nor crowned, nor need he lose his strength and fall
Along the road, but that he bore a cross
And was like many more that had been called
And loved. A thief, she'd heard it said, a thief
Who was to die for what he had not gained.
They'd caught him. He had not smelled innocent.
And they had braced him with his fellow, struck
Swift judgment, and had sent him on to make
Rare company for Him Who also was
To die, and Who would not be strange to thieves.
She'd known that he was there, and now his voice
Was falling, and the tone of it had caught
Within her. He was twisting, speaking out.

And we indeed justly, for we receive the due reward of our deeds: but this man hath done no evil. And he said to Jesus: Lord, remember me when thou shalt come into thy kingdom.

She did not need to hope He'd make response.
This pleading was enough. This deference,
This fealty that fell so strangely down
Among the tangled curses and could give
A sudden lifting in surprise to pain,
This word that moved her swiftly to another
Cross than His, that warmed her in the cold
Abundance of denials, this defeat
Of time, already claimed its own conclusion,
And she knew it was already answered.

And Jesus said to him: Amen I say to thee, this day thou shalt be with me in paradise.

Again we find that it is Luke who writes
These words that others have not written down.
They're saved for us. She'd have us know He spoke.
However she had listened, we are sure
He'd made an answer. She was there. She heard.

We are not always made aware this day
Was blackened in a night that came too soon.
We somehow seem to miss the simple fact
He died in darkness, and that shadows came
Upon the light, and crept across the skies
Like slow, encroaching wings to spread a horror
On the earth and doubting fear. We do
Not always see that in the frames the masters
Left us there is night on Calvary.
But it was so, and if we search again
Among the pages that are ours to read
For record, we will find it; darkness fallen
On the earth; and from the sixth hour till
The ninth a darkness cloaked and covered Him.
And afterward we note a sudden ceasing
Of the curses that had been so full
And confident before. Aye, once we mark
It, it is strange how sharp the ending comes
To all derision. There is word of dark,
And then we do not find them tempting Him.
As if they feared. As if they stole away
To distance, leaving space about His feet.
Because they feared. Because they were not sure.
Not sure. And had no more of blustering
Contempt to laugh to Him upon His cross.
And suddenly young John can look about
And find there are not many he might name.

Now there stood by the cross of Jesus, his mother and his mother's sister, Mary of Cleophas, and Mary Magdalen.

A little knot of women. Only these
To watch the slow hours out and to remain
Of all who'd come to Him upon so many
Other hillsides, and who had protested
They'd not go away, and who had said
He should be king. John counts them. They are few,
Like remnants standing of a kingdom now
Dissolved, like lost, bewildered, emptied souls
Left weeping when a day had grown to dark
And all hosannahs had been long abandoned
To a past. John names them. He has time
To see they are not many clustered here.

The wind moves torpidly upon the hill,
And puffs the dust to languid whirls that rise
And fall again, and in the dark her veils
Are stirring and the wind is hot across
Her face, and she is lonely as her life
Had ever been. John does not say she cried,
Or that she leaned upon another's breast
For ease, or that she came so near she might
Have touched His feet, or kissed them, or embraced
Him in some comfort He might have or she
Might have in that they were not separate,
And that their human needs and loves and bonds
Were strong and had endured and still were whole
To them. He does not say she moved or swayed
For sorrow. John, young John who met her first
So long ago at Cana and had not

Forgotten how she turned and looked to him,
And what the search had been beneath her eyes,
Young John who had discovered then the flame
To whiteness burning and had known her in
An instant, and whose soul had claimed its need
And had been claimed in kin and recognition
Sealed between them, John who loved her so,
Who was so swift in wisdom, says no more
Than that she only stood beneath His cross.

And afterward he tells in simple statement
What he heard and what it was he saw.

When Jesus therefore had seen his mother and the disciple standing, whom he loved, he said to his mother: Woman, behold thy son. After that, he saith to the disciple: Behold thy mother. And from that hour the disciple took her to his own.

She was aware then of His long look falling
Down. She felt His gaze, His contemplation
Strong at last, and certain, held to her.
Beyond the thieves, the crowds, the hill, beyond
The bite of thorns and past the stretched, consuming
Burn of nails, beyond the laboring
And swell of breath, the heat, the sweat, the stench,
Beyond the shattering and reel of pain,
John says He found her, that He strained in sight
And saw her there. And could she be unsure
He saw? In any weariness or grief
Was there enough she would not feel His eyes
And know that for unfaltered moment now
He found, and recognized and gave to her

A long regard? She knew. She knew that He
Had seen, and for the space of while He bent
To her, an old world rose again and they
Were two at Nazareth. This was the last.
The far sweet history had come to ending,
And He searched to seek her for a final
Instant. There will be no more for Him,
Or her. This was the end, the last resumption
And the last accord of all the rich
Days running in the past to infancy.
He will not look again, nor will He lift
His voice to call or speak to her again.
This was the end. Relinquishment. Surrender,
And a long dismissal made complete
In one remembering and dear renewal
Of the years that are unraveled now
And done. She'd known this was to be, that soon
Would be a last time, and she'd give Him then
To death, that she would come to Him, and in
Some definite and certain moment, find
She'd spent the last of life and that beyond
No more remained, and He'd not see, or know,
Or speak to her again. And now she stood
Upon this other side of certitude,
And had no more of time, and held Him all
In memory.

When Jesus therefore had seen his mother . . . he said to his mother: Woman, behold thy son. After that, he saith to the disciple: Behold thy mother.

The sounding of His words
Repeated and returned within her when

He'd done with speaking, and His parched lips closed.
Returned. Returned within her. Over. Over.
"Son. Thy mother." He was saying . . . "Woman.
Son. Thy mother." And His meaning, bent
And dark, and poised above the pain, descended
On her in demand so huge, so weighed,
She found her instant summoning of answer
Could not be, save in the whole bequeathing
Of her heart to void, and in complete
Oblation that should leave no more of her.
He'd asked He be to her no longer son!

He'd severed her from Him! He'd asked not tears,
Nor pain, nor life, He'd asked she turn away
From motherhood! That she unbind her bond
In Him, deny her name, her love, refuse
Her own and grant that He was not and she
No longer be! By will and wish and prayer,
He'd asked that she undo Him, break, O, break
Her love, to give it back and let Him bleed
The rest of sacrifice uncomforted,
Untended and alone. He'd reached to last
Bleak bitter edges and His hour had come.
He'd strike her separate and be abandoned!
She must turn from Him, and must accept
Another son that had not been her own.
Behold. Behold thy mother. This *thy* mother
Here! She'd heard His words and stood beneath
Them and did not refuse, nor fail, nor cry.
John, young John, remembers she was standing
So. And was a woman: crushed in silence
And the pain of silence was her heart
That gave no more, since there was nothing more.

Remaining time to death thereafter was
Not wait or watch for her. He had already
Died. He'd gone from her. More certainly,
And by a farther width than merely death
Has coldness or deceit to give, He'd gone
From her. He'd said He was no longer hers.
He'd given her denial and had turned
Away the one claim earth might keep of Him
That was unsoiled and unalloyed, and He
Was hanging, stripped and bleeding, and alone!
In pain, as if there never had been she
To lean above His crib, as if her hands
Had not unfolded swaddling bands, and He'd
Not ever rested hiding in her womb.
He hung here, motherless, alone, alone.
For she had heard Him speak and she had willed
Her heart to be the crumbling of an ash,
To be destroyed, to be unflamed of Him!
She had obeyed. She'd seen this pain, this woundless
Martyrdom, she'd looked within to this,
His uttered and His full intent, and she
Had answered. It was done to her according
To His word: and she had lost a Son,
And John might wear His childhood as his own.

The darkness rising like a thickened mist
Had covered Him, and voices softened down
To harsh, infrequent whisperings that bore
An evidence of awe. They felt the rumbles
Of unquiet in the earth. The sky
Was altered and the monstrous threat of evil
Moved upon it like a fear, and huge,
Enormous dread lay clouded on the world.

He was a figure, lonely, lost, aloof
Upon His cross, and in His pain, and He
Had gone beyond the reach of human ease
And for some lengthened moments now, He had
Not raised His head, or moaned, or seemed to live.
She watched Him, and around her, she could feel
The deadened hush and all the clinging eyes
That looked to Him and waited for His death.
They were around her, heavy, near, and pressed
Together in a throng where He was lifted
Up, and was so broken and so torn.
He had not moved, and then His breath was gasped
In sudden need, His breast heaved laboring,
His arms were tightened, and His bended face
Was swung and tortured upward to the dark.
He cried, this cry, aloud. She heard Him sob
In jagged pain, as if He'd lost His soul
And cried in anguish from the rims of hell!

My God, my God, why hast thou forsaken me?

An utter coldness knifed across her mind
And left her numbed and shivering. His cry!
She stared to Him, her eyes distended, wide.
His cry! His cry! She had not heard *that* anguish
Wrung upon His voice before! His cry!
The drawn and piercing cry that cut to her,
That she could recognize by sound and strength
And accent as His own, but as the pleading
Of a stranger in a pain He could
Not know! The screech that is the cry of evil
Seen and borne, the last abandonment
That is the night, the burned, the final touch

And emptiness of loss, dark desolation,
Closed and made complete! O, He had gone
From her and turned within to keep alone
The task He'd pledged. She'd heard Him will that *she*
Forsake Him. But this cry, this other cry . . .

Sometime a man named Paul will write a page
And send it out to cities and to shores
She will not see. And Paul will keep an insight
That will dare to let him write of this
And of this cry. And he will say of Him
He knew a curse, that He was ours, and hanging
On a tree became for us, accursed!

Afterward she sensed a change in Him,
As if He'd gone the whole way of His pain,
And there was little more for His endurance,
And not much of time until the end.
She felt the running of a swifter movement
In events, some inner hastening
That need not linger now and sought to find
Finality. She knew too much of all
The forms of anguish to mistake the barb
That caused His sobbing and the broken cry.
An ultimate had touched Him, and beyond,
No more remained for Him, no further depth,
Nor bitterness, nor any sharper sorrow
That He still must seek and make His own.
She recognized that He had met the full
Exaction, and a hundred or a thousand
Torments in the nails could add no measure
More, and only be a lesser pain
Than He had suffered in abandonment.

She'd lost Him once, she'd known forsakenness,
And when He'd cried aloud and she had heard,
She had some judgment to assay what end,
What exquisite and utter consummation
He had reached, and now, her pulses raced
Again, and she could feel beneath the dark,
The rush and nearness of an instant signed
And waited since eternity, and cupped
In her as in a chalice since she'd turned
To Him to be the bearer of His life
And of His death.

He had subsided now,
And He was quieter and tensions strung
In Him had been released, and He was wearied
In an after listlessness and almost
As a man who could remember nothing
More, who had no strength to give in long
Resistance, He had murmured of His body's
Need, and spoken helplessly of need.

I thirst.

She watched them moving, and could hear them say
In jest perhaps Elias would descend
To comfort Him, but one of them could take
The blessing of a gratitude within
Her eyes. He jested too, this nameless man
That she must hold forever in her love,
He jested too, but in defence of pity;
And she saw him lift a dripping sponge
That He might drink.

There was a new intentness
Drawn in her, a tightened and increased
Observing, and a watch to Him made taut
And more unwavered since she knew His heart
Was straining, and the beat and pace of blood
Were throbbing to an end that was not far.
Her hands pressed whiter in the veils, and she
Was fixed immovably to see, to see
The sign that would be soon upon His face.
Her own heart pounded, and her throat was dry.
She waited Him and felt the others move
To her and cluster for a close protection
Near.

He spoke and on His voice was meaning
She'd not be the last to understand.

It is consummated.

How much, and of what length of dreams and hopes
And sorrows, of what plans and destinies
Laid deep beneath the slow repeating years,
And guided up to this, their pinnacle
And end; what laughter sounding in the summer's
Sun; what race and tumult of a boy's
Young gladness; what of glimpses and perceiving
Opened suddenly to pain; what ache
Of childhood reaching to her; what of prayers,
Departures, tears and laboring, and what
Of gain and triumph carried on His breath
And summed forever, only she who was
So silent, standing silent, only she

Could know. And what of love He said had come
To perfecting. They had not failed, aye, they,
They had not failed. She'd borne His Calvary.
This too was hers. Her own. His totaling
And word of full conclusion could be hers,
And He could speak for her. In humbleness
And in the unabashed and simple daring
Of the truth, she knew she was not absent
From His speech. A consummation. Hers.

And Jesus crying with a loud voice, said: Father, into thy hands I commend my spirit. And saying this he gave up the ghost.

* * * *

And all the world was gone and she was left
Among the shadows of an emptied earth,
And in a nothingness. There were no sounds,
Nor sights, nor movements. There was nothing now.
No ground, nor quaking in the ground, no dark,
Nor cries, nor sobbing close to her. There were
No gathered groups that turned away with fear
Upon them and with hands that beat their breasts.
There was no wind, nor heat, nor tired ache,
And only there was nothingness, and He
Who was a grey face staring out of sightless
Eyes. The substance and the forms of solid
Things had gone, the meaning of her breath;
There was no time, nor place, but only He
Who did not move but hung so still, so limp,

So heavied on the nails. She saw Him. Dead.
Dead! A body that was drained of life.
His pain had ceased. It came to her His pain
Had ended and that more of agony
Should not be in His limbs. He would not cry
Again or thirst or need to hold Himself
For longer bearing of the opened wounds.
The pain too, that had died.

He was not there.
He'd left them. They were all alone. Alone.
She was all alone. She saw Him. There.
His head, His features that had shone with life,
With answers; and His feet, His feet that she
Had washed and strapped in sandals and had waited,
Listening. She saw Him. But He was
Not there. She could not look to Him and find
Him. There was no place on the earth where she
Could find Him, and she could not close her eyes
And think again, as she had done, that He
Was in this place or that, that He was walking
Here, or there, on this, or other roads,
Or on a shore, or field, or hill . . . but near.
And sure, for all the distances, so sure.
This was the first time. She was strange in it,
And hushed for it was new. This was the first
Time she was utterly alone, alone,
With nowhere she could think to, or could hope,
Or ask to be. No place where she could say
It was obedience for her to be
Not there. He'd gone from earth. He'd gone. He'd
died.

The rush and surge and sudden certainty
Were waves within her beating in her mind,
And falling in impress and ebb and press
Of truth that swelled and rolled to her, engulfing,
Passing, rising . . . He had gone. He'd gone.
He was not there. She looked to Him. The tumult
And the throng, the hill, the shouts, the dark
Had vanished, there was only He. His wounds,
His riven hands, the shape, the red of Him,
The opened mouth so loosened and so dark.
There was only He, Who did not live.

She need no longer ponder prophecies.
They were too plain before her and were filled
With all accomplishment, and she might see
The troubled dreams Isaias had made real.
The sombre singing of the psalms had come
To Him, and she had heard them out to ending.
In Him now their sadness had been turned
And was a past. The deep hour that had brooded
On His Name was done. She was a witness
To fulfillment, and the sure awareness
Told that time had crossed a boundary,
And she was living in the first of moments
In a newer time. He was a Will
That now no longer needed to be done.
She knew the meaning that was cut forever
On her heart, this cross, this broken Man,
This offering concluded and complete.
He'd met His whole of sorrow, and there was
No more for Him to give. She knew Him here.
His love had taken Him at last, and squandered
Him!

A fear, and some sharp new concern
Upon the voices speaking all around
Her, rose and reached to her, and she was drawn
From Him; and in a quickened and aroused
Attention, searched the voices and the words
They had to say. There were so many here.
She found them, friends, His friends who had been in
The throng and who had stood afar from Him,
And women, followers from Galilee,
They were around her now. She saw them, moving
In, with tears not dry upon their cheeks,
And speaking in the worried tones of new
Anxiety. They looked to Him, and she
Could hear and take from them the fear they spoke
About His body now. What disposition
Would be made of Him? Who'd take Him down?
Who'd dare to claim Him, to assert a need
For other burial than thieves might have?
She had not thought of that, that at the end
She'd have no certain right to care for Him,
That even death would not return Him hers,
That He was still condemned, and was but One
Beside two others who were also slain,
That He'd be cast with them into a common
Place, some pit, some trench, that would be dug
And covered over with the careless earth,
Anonymous and scorned.

Until a man
Who wore the fringes of the Sanhedrin
Was strangely there among them at His cross.
He was not poor. He had not come with them
From Galilee, nor had he been accounted

One who'd be expected to appear
At this place in a grief that was not feigned.
But he was there, and she had heard his good
Devotion speak a favor he would ask
Of Pilate, that might give Him back to them
That they might make a kingdom of His grave.

It is not written down nor anywhere
Recorded she had noticed that the name
He had was Joseph, that this man who came
With counsel on his lips and with decision
In a plan to give to their distress,
With strength for them, this man had not a strange
Name that she did not know. They called him Joseph,
And in that he was a hope for her,
And left a confidence when he had gone.

We seldom think of time continuing
Beyond His death and of the after hours
That were as slow for her and were as long
As she'd endured before the silence came
About Him, and a peace was sealed upon
His lips. But she was not released to any
Sphere that was aloof from pain and ache
And dust and waiting, and where all confusion
And the loosened scattering of movements
In a crisis ended, were not swung
Around her. She was standing on a hill
Where crucifixion had been done, and if
He'd died, His hands were still beneath the nails,
And in His feet, the nails. They'd not dissolved.
A cross struck upright in the earth, and soaked
Beneath a man's blood does not fade away

To air, nor offer quietly a soft
Escape for one who sees and one who loves.

And there was time here. She was still in time.
Supposing Joseph in his rank and with
Prestige to aid him, had so hurried on
To gain a swift permission and had turned
With spices purchased and with linens bought,
And made no lingering and no delay,
It still would be an hour's length and more,
Before she saw him and could hear what word
He had. And this was anguish. This was fear,
And doubt, uncertainty. She did not know.
She was not sure His body, cut and torn,
And hanging there, so sacred, so beloved,
So near, she was not sure they might release
Him, take Him down, and have Him for their own.
Such grief, and loss, as we can only measure
Distantly and guess at in a dim
Appraisal of her pain, such utter sorrow
As might seek the faint relief of tears,
And ask now only to be left to mourn,
Such freedom as abandonment might give
To be alone in, even this could not
Be hers. She was not free. She was not now
Unshadowed and unheld. She had not done
With fears, or darker threats, or thrusts that still
Might strike to her. This was an hour burdened
With a questioned grave, and long with wait,
And sharpened in unease and in the need
To hold Him in her arms. She'd be a couch
For Him, she'd take Him, fold Him, care for Him,
She'd bathe His blistered shoulders, keep a watch,

And in her heartbreak, guard Him to a humble
Place where He might be, and be her own
Who was discharged of nails, and thorns, and timbers
Laid on Him. She'd turn to Him. She'd bring . . .
But we must not forget that for a whole
And bitter length of time she did not know
What more would reach to Him, or what event
Might fall to take Him from her, shattered now
In death.

There were enough of threats and hard,
Ungentle menacings to make the fears
In her so real she could not find assurance
They were only fears, and that a little
More of wait would make an end of them.
She must have heard debate and reference
Around her of the law, and been aware
They spoke of Him, when it was said this body
With the others might become a scandal
Touching on the Sabbath and a stain
Upon the air. She must have sensed this purpose
To dispose of scandals and observed
Them hastening away to say to Pilate
That he should be swift in his dispatch,
And that their Sabbath fell at evening.
She waited here. She could not seek or touch
Or hold Him. She must wait here. Wait. And Joseph
Had not yet returned. She did not know.
And when the strain of time had drawn in her
To longer waiting, then she saw the soldiers
Come again, and after blunt, efficient
Orders that had not been paused to count
If any wept, or any mourned, she watched

Them group about the crosses: and the thud
Of clubs was sickened on the heavied air,
And two who had been caught in crime were dead.
They turned to Him! She saw them and she did
Not cry, or scream to them, or is there page
To tell she moved, or grew more faint, or called
Protesting. John is scrupulous to write
That he must be believed, that what he saw
Was not imagined, that he truly saw,
And John does not declare she faltered then
For grief, or fear, or even that she cried.
And we may only know that she endured
A last wound fastened to the wounds He wore
For utter seal, and final poverty.

But one of the soldiers with a spear opened his side, and immediately there came out blood and water.

The word had come to her that they had done
With Him, and laws were done, and courts and kings.
They'd make no further claim. It was reported
He was dead, that He was mangled, dumb
Of mouth, and broken in His pride, and that
His head hung movelessly. They had no use
Or other need of Him, and whosoever
Wished might let Him down and look to Him.
The law released Him. Pilate set Him free.

And now we are so sure. This moment now.
We are so sure. Her hands were lifted up
Like hands that pray, like hands that reach a love
Grown infinite beyond all other sign,
And slowly, exquisite in soul, and softly,

They unloosed and lowered Him, and gave
Him back to be within her arms. She took
Him then. His mother. She accepted Him,
And they were silent in the awe that she,
Receiving Him, should be so stilled. The stripes
Along His back were circled now and hid.
She held Him, folded Him. His thorns were taken,
Tangled in His hair, she touched, untwisting
Them, and freed His head to find an old
Place on her breast. And in a long, unsobbed,
And slow accounting, she looked down the wounds
And saw them near, that were so dark and endless
To His feet. This was the lash that streaked
Him. She had heard the lash and had already
Known its pain. But she could see now. Scars.
Cut in upon Him. Visible. And deep.
She could remember how His spread hand rested
So against her when she'd sung to Him.
He had been fair, and easily He'd smiled
Beneath His sleep, and she had hugged the warm
Weight close to her. She could remember now.
He had been fair, and whole, and warm, and she
Did not then have a coldness in her moving
To His cold. And when the world and time
Returned, and she could feel them come to her,
And heard them ask for Him, her fingers closed
On Him defending, and her arms were strong,
And for an instant, held. And then she looked
To find that Joseph bending to her, had
No words to say, and tears were in his eyes.
She had been lost. She had been rocking Him.

* * * *

Death brings a kindness and the griefs that rise
Of it are never left to ask unoffered
Aid. And this was more than death: and many
Who had learned and found a life in Him
Were eager. John recalls that Nicodemus
Gave a hundredweight of myrrh, and Joseph
Said there was a tomb he owned not far
From here, that it was new, and they might reach
To it before the dark.

She watched them washing
Him, and did not need to speak of care
Or reverence. She may have held a band
Of linen while they wound Him silently.
Or moved among them, quiet, frail, the years,
The long, long years upon her, and the lines
Deep creased beneath her eyes, she may have moved
To Him, and touched Him, only touched Him now,
And crossed His hands, and looked on Him again,
And sobless, stooped to place on Him her kiss.

They covered Him, and were so swift against
The coming Sabbath that the women spoke
Of incompletion, and a heedful love
As yet unsatisfied. He was a white
Form lying still upon the ground. She saw
Him. Still. His heart unbeating. Still. Beneath
The cloth His face that did not feel the cloth
Unmoving. Here. A white form lying here.

And somewhere near to Him, she walked away
From Calvary. She walked the earth again,
And turned away and found the slopes that led

Descending down this hill where she had died.
She followed Him, and they were figures stealing
In the gloom around a white form, silent
To their tears. John. And Magdalen.
The others. They were there. And men who carried
Him. But she was walking now. Alone.
His hour had come and she had seen it pass.
And she was walking here. She was alone.

And Joseph . . . laid him in a sepulchre, which was hewed out of a rock. And he rolled a stone to the door of the sepulchre.

Jerusalem preparing for the Pasch
Was filled with guests and was absorbed in old
And usual observances. And lights
Were springing up, and high above the walls
The Temple waited, and a teeming city
Flowed and spread beneath.

She turned to leave.
A woman in the dusk before a tomb.
Her veils were on her and her step was slow,
And looking, she could see upon a hill
A cross stabbed upright in the earth, as if
It were a sword that should not be withdrawn.
She paused a moment. But there was no need
Or reason now for her to stay. She knew.
This was an ended cross and was a past.
She was a woman who had borne a Son.
This was a cross. And on it He had died.

XVI

THIS day that could not be, had waited them,
They found, beyond a sudden dawn, so clear,
So new, so unbelievable, they woke
To it with only sadness in their eyes,
And sorrow lifting up to search for more
Of tears. They did not know. They did not rouse
To quick expectancy, nor turn before
The east to drink the light in for a draught
That spilled to them and was His own to give.
They were not certain, running in the dews
To where they'd laid Him and a stone was rolled,
Nor were they murmurous with little laughters
For the guards. They woke to only night,
And to a third day breaking in the pain.

We find them moving, sadly, anxiously,
These women with the spices and the oils
Of more anointing. They are closed within
The dark: Salome, Mary Cleophas,
Johanna, moving out to seek again
His tomb, concerned for Him. They had not done
With all of care His body might have had.
They are in haste, and with them, Magdalen.
We find them so, these women who had loved
And followed Him, but tracing down the few
Accounted names, and searching in the lists
Remembered and recorded, we do not
Discover she was there. We do not find

Her name. She is not mentioned, she who stood
Until His last pain passed from Him, who had
Not failed, nor flagged, nor ever made delay
To any need in all His years, she was
Not there, who gave Him birth, who is His mother,
Was not there!

We sense the loss of her,
The lack. This is omission. Vacancy.
A name unsaid that we had grown so used
To hearing we are left unsatisfied,
As if a strong and waited reference
Does not befall.

The rest is clear to us;
The frightened, spreading, swift dismay of these
First hours is as plain as if the shock
Of His untenanted and emptied tomb
Had come to us, and it had been our eyes
That saw He lay not there. Magdalen
Is trembling in return. She had gone on
Beyond the rest, impatient, searching Him,
And now, she runs here trembling in return.
Across the fields, the grass, the gates, the streets,
To cry to Peter of a dark invasion
Of His grave. She'd seen an empty place!
He lay not there! She speaks. Of broken seals,
The stone removed, the grey and gaping sight
That loomed before her in the mists of morning.
And the emptiness! He lay not there!

Young John and Peter, startled, hurrying
In answer. It is plain to us. They stand

Before the entrance and a fear is hard
Upon their throats. The stone had been removed!
They do not speak. And silently they stoop
Within and stare together at the cloths
That had been wound on Him, and at the folded
Veil! They knew. They had been lost in grief,
And they had not remembered. Now they knew!

And in distinctness we have kept a clear
And later utterance these women heard
Who only came to minister to death.

They saw a young man sitting on the right side, clothed with a white robe: and they were astonished. Who saith to them: Be not affrighted; you seek Jesus of Nazareth, who was crucified: he is risen, he is not here, behold the place where they laid him.

And we can understand the chaos left
To them, this shattering by blunt reversal
Of accustomed order they must grasp
And tell to others in a language fitted
To a tale impossible. We sense
Belief, and unbelief, a news confirmed,
Refused, confirmed again, the fear, the quick
Debates that ended in a fresh recounting
To another who had come because
He'd heard and did not dare to think he'd heard.
We need not more than what is written down
To find confusion and too sudden joy.

And we can know that Magdalen might follow
After John and Peter and remain

To weep and be alone when they had gone.
The sequence in events is clear to us.
She marks the treading of a Gardener
Who comes to walk the earth as One Who had
Been here before. She cries to Him a fear,
And in the hush of morning, quietly,
A Voice is asking her: "Why weepest thou?"

This wonder and this clear, upyielding joy,
Uncaptive, free, and new upon the tears
Of loss, still sounds in all the triumph bells
We ring, and in the peal of trumpet lilies
That we gather up to stand among
Our songs. This still is shouting in our Spring.
We have not lost His accent of return.
We listen yet and hear the quivered air
Take up the sounding of His voice to carry
It in limpid waves along the far
Receiving skies until the whole of air
Is new and silvered in the breath of Him.
This dawn that cannot be, and is, still lights
For us. We have not grown too gross with years,
Nor dull with other deaths to keep this day
And trace again the first fresh news of it.

But when we turn to search among the glad
Reportings, and the running feet, some word
Of her, some sign, or phrase, or memory
To tell that she was eager in this dawn,
And found swift joy and sudden ecstasy
Released to her, that He should be, and be
Returned, that He was living, speaking out
Again to them with life within His eyes,

When we would look for her, to cry our gladness
That she need not weep beside His tomb,
We find she is not here. She was not seeking
With the rest. She is not named with them,
Nor is there word she walked before the light
To search His body and to care for Him.

And are we then to think she did not feel
This need as others? That some negligence
Or confidence in tombs had come to her
To make her judge a hasty burial
Had been enough for Him? May we conclude
That she was satisfied and did not find
An urge to move again in ministry?
That all her tears were shed, and she had made
An end of tears? Had such a weariness
Been swathed about her, she had changed, and these
Were not as three days once had been within
Her heart? Or could it be young John had not
Remembered she was there, and merely had
Not named her, and that in his ears the voice
Of last commission given him had dulled
So soon and he'd not noticed her? Was she
Asleep and heavied in the night when they
Were stirring up in eagerness?

Or is
It truer thought of her she found no need
To search? And better said that she had known
Within, they'd not discover Him again
Among the dead? That He would not be there
Entombed, and she had known, and only watched
Them now as they were whispering of Him,

And let them go, and listened afterward
To footsteps that were fading in the dark.

To wait Him here. Alone. Alone. A woman
Lonely in the silence and the trust
Of silence is her heart that did not seek,
Or cry, or search, but only waited Him.

We have no word of this sweet certainty
That hides in her. There is not granted line
Writ meagre in the scripture that will tell
By even some poor, unavailing tag
Of language what she keeps within the silence.
This is hers. We are not told of this,
This quaking instant, this return, this Light
Beyond the tryst of dawn when she first lifted
Up her eyes, and quiet, unamazed,
Saw He was near. This is her own, this moment
When He came, as always Nazareth
Will be her own, and all the secrets hid
Beneath the long years' long remembering.
We may not guess His countenance that looked
Again upon her after Calvary,
When He could find her old with what had passed,
And worn with it, and on her brow, the deep
Lines cut forever unobliterate
And dark. We may not know what words He said,
Or whether He had any use or need
In words, nor may we dare to think what tears
For her were brimming of His love. He raised
His hands to touch again her hair, and let
Her feel the weight again of life in Him?

He showed the wounds and offered them, a sign
Of whole accomplishment? He moved to her?
He was a good Son come again? Released
To be her own, and in this hidden quiet,
Freed of reticence and all retentions
That the years had held in Him when still
A cross must be? She was beyond the cross.
Past threat and wait for it. She'd given Him.
And now He was returned. She spoke His name?
And cried? Or did she only see the Light
That never was invisible to her,
Effulgent, shining on His face in first
Forever, lighting by a clear and dimless
Radiance, the past, the pains, the words
He'd said, and what she'd done, and what her part
Had been, and falling now on her for peace
And for finality? And was she claimed
By strong and utter joy to give a nearer
Adoration to His heart? Her spirit's
New magnificat that is rejoiced
Again because He hath regarded her,
And holy is His name?

Or was she only
Quieted in simple sight of Him,
And eased again that He might be with her,
And not ecstatic, awed, or startled now,
But only eased, and in the silence, grateful
He had done with pain, and need endure
No more, and that the distance of His death
Had ended, and that living He had come
To her?

When Peter summoned them to tell
In quivered speech his eyes had looked on Him
And with his own ears he had heard the living
Sound, they must have turned away to fill
The day again with ardent, new detailing;
That He lived; that He'd appeared to Peter
With His body whole. And she had learned
Again of Him, from someone, John, or others,
Come to her to bring new confirmations
Peter gave. And she was unamazed,
And quiet, listening, O, listening
Of Him!

Two men who had been on a road
Came back to cry that He had walked with them.
Had sat at table and had broken bread,
And that they knew Him so, in forms of bread
That He had broken.

And when evening
Had come to close this day, John might have had
A longer word to bring to where she was,
A word that needed moments for a longer
Telling, and that might be hers to hold
For deeper meanings vibrant on his voice,
And with old love to take the place of fear.
They had been gathered in a room behind
Some doors. They were afraid. And in the midst
Of them, He stood, and spoke of peace to them.
He'd breathed upon their faces with His breath.
John will remember that, that on his face
He'd felt a moist breath, close and warm with life,
And looked upon Him from no further distance

Than a breath. And He was long with them.
And kind. He'd said to them they might forgive . . .
For Him.

But this was not the old ways come
Again. She knew that. He had not returned.
His presence might be here, or there. They'd see
Him. He was living. He was on the earth
And real, and He had moved again to plans
And to directions. He would speak with them,
And touch them out of sorrow and defeat
Their grief. It should be clear to them the nailed
Feet trod upon the dust to leave imprinting
Plain. He'd give commands and make summation.
They should hear of Him. But He had not
Returned. She knew that. He would not resume
As if He had not died, and Nazareth
And Bethany and all the green hills rising,
And the fields were ended. He had done
With them, and she would not have more to take
For sweetness and an old simplicity
Regained. He was not given back to her,
Nor ever would be. Time was past her now.
He'd come. She'd held Him in her arms and cared
For Him. He'd grown, and then she'd watched the swift
Years falling, and He'd gone away. The pain
Of share in Him had twisted in her heart.
And now He'd died. The wounds were on Him, sealed
And shining. She had seen Him. He had come
Again, and fire was running on the earth,
He was alive, but He was not returned.
She knew that now. She'd seen Him, but He'd not

Returned. His name had altered. He had gone.
He was beyond the hold of any hearth
Or need or place or time. He was her own.
That still was true. But He was not returned.

There was some pause within Jerusalem,
A little while of lingering that held
An evidence for Thomas, and the words
He cried in answer. There was some delay,
Some tarrying, and then we find them come
Again to Galilee: and we may guess
That she had gone with them, and in the long
Return, came lonely to the paths of home.
She had no reason or a love to raise
Reluctance at departure. This was not
For her a city that had been so kind
She might not leave without regret or loss
Or eagerness to be afar from it.
These streets were not unfilled with memory,
Nor had they been so generous to her
She'd not be grateful for a span of absence
And not seeing them. And John had gone.
She must stay now with John, and when we read
Of Galilee, and that they hauled the nets
Again along familiar shores, and launched
The boats again, we may be sure that somewhere
She was near, and moved again among
The faces she had known. And He had known.

And waiting for her here in Galilee
The first faint cast of final loneliness
Was like a cold light paling that need not
Be seen as yet since she could feel it fallen

On this land. She'd have no cause to go
From here, no place to look to or to think
She might soon seek in coming time. These were
The hills without Him now. These were His roads
Without the hope that He might pass, or turn
A lane to bring a shadow in this sun.
This was the world without Him, after Him,
The silence when His words had all been said,
And He had gone. This was her own place, lonely,
And she'd come to it.

O, we can keep
No surety He did not visit her,
That never in these brief days did He speak
In secret, coming to her as the ease
Of quiet prayer. She may have found Him more
Than is recorded or revealed to us.
We have no right to vision, nor enough
Of sanctity to dare behold. We.do
Not know. He came to Peter and to John
Along the lake and was a simple friend
To them, Who sought to please them with a leisure
And with good words spoken as they sat
And ate together of a fish He'd broiled.
Paul says He spoke to hundreds on a hill.
And He could not have been less generous
With her. Would He not come to her for length
And ease with quietness and hide another
Nazareth we do not see?

And when
H'd gone again beyond the bonds of space
And time, and Galilee was only land

Again upon a vacant world, could she
Not feel the loneliness? And wait for Him.

It was not long before they left the nets,
And moving on, as men who keep appointment,
Turned again unto Jerusalem.
We find them so, and in His last word's fall,
They are not far from where the Temple roofs
Are gold and gleaming in a burnished signal
To the sun. And did she go with John?
Or was it only later that her feet
Sought roads again and wandered to the house
That had an upper room?

She stood upon
The earth. She was yet here. Somewhere. Somewhere,
She was on the earth. And then they brought
Her news. Upon a day set definite
And certain in the slow, anonymous
Repeating host of days, they came to bring
A news that she must hear. *They could not look
For Him again. He'd left them. He was gone!*

The wide arc of an empty sky was curving
Over her and over far horizons.
She could trace the bend and sweep of it,
And followed down its fall of utter silence,
Till it closed around her on the rims
Of earth and was a circle, stilled, complete.
She was alone. He would not come to her
Again. She moved a little, and the sound
Of movement lifted up against the day
And fell, and did not rise. She was alone,

And in her she could feel the flow of time
That had begun and would go on, go on,
To days, in silence, on and on. She was
A woman now who was alone with time,
And in her heart, the wait and ache of time.

January 4, 1941.

BIBLIOGRAPHY

AND ACKNOWLEDGMENT

The few passages in the text that vary from the authority of the New Testament narrative are clearly indicated. There is one exception: the name of Joachim is known only to tradition and is used in the First Episode without introduction.

The Scriptural quotations are all from the Douay Version of the Bible.

The sources for the chronology, details of background, motivation, geographical details, etc., are the following works: *Jesus Christ* by Père Didon, *O.P.; The Life of Christ* by Mgr. E. Le Camus; *The Life and Teaching of Jesus Christ* by Jules Lebreton, S.J.; the three volumes of illustrations by J. James Tissot; a dissertation on *The Boyhood Consciousness of Christ* by Rev. Patrick J. Temple, S.T.L.; *The Christ the Son of God* by Abbé Constant Fouard, from which came suggestions embodied in the Thirteenth Episode; and, especially, the excellent and satisfactory two volumes titled *The Gospel of Jesus Christ* by Père M. J. La Grange, O.P.

I am very much indebted to Father James M. McGlinchey, C.M., of the ever charitable Vincentian Fathers for his careful reading of these pages, and for the corrections that he submitted to bring the work scrupulously within the limits of what is factually contained in the New Testament.

NIHIL OBSTAT: Vincent M. Mayer, O.M.C., Censor Librorum.

IMPRIMATUR: ✠ Walter A. Foery, D.D.
Bishop of Syracuse.

Syracuse, N.Y. May 10, 1941.